Chaos to Clarity

Chaos to Clarity

Making Sense of Complex Business Transformation

Caren Shiozaki

Chaos to Clarity:
Making Sense of Complex Business Transformation

Copyright © Business Expert Press, LLC, 2026.

Cover design by Hannah Feldman

Interior design by S4Carlisle Publishing Services, Chennai, India

All rights reserved. No part of this publication may be reproduced, stored in a retrieval system, or transmitted in any form or by any means—electronic, mechanical, photocopy, recording, or any other except for brief quotations, not to exceed 400 words, without the prior permission of the publisher.

First published in 2026 by
Business Expert Press, LLC
222 East 46th Street, New York, NY 10017
www.businessexpertpress.com

ISBN-13: 978-1-60649-184-3 (paperback)
ISBN-13: 978-1-60649-275-8 (e-book)

Service Systems and Innovations for Business and Society Collection

First edition: 2026
10 9 8 7 6 5 4 3 2 1

EU SAFETY REPRESENTATIVE
Mare Nostrum Group B.V.
Doelen 72
4831 GR Breda
The Netherlands
gpsr@mare-nostrum.co.uk

Description

Chaos to Clarity: Making Sense of Complex Business Transformation is an essential guide for leaders who must navigate the intersection of strategy, people, process, and technology change.

Written in clear, executive-level language, this book demystifies complex business transformation as a holistic reinvention of how an organization creates value, engages customers, and operates in today's volatile and fast-moving business environment.

Through practical frameworks that the author has applied in real-world situations, readers explore the key dimensions of transformation—process redesign, technology modernization, organizational structure, and cultural evolution—while addressing common challenges such as workforce readiness, change resistance, governance, and risk.

This book is intended for executives and senior leaders, to help them understand the "why," "what," and "how" of complex business transformation. It provides advice on preparing for implementation success and establishing governance to promote accountability and strategic alignment.

Finally, this book enables leaders to lead with clarity and confidence to reshape their businesses not just for today's competitive pressures but for a sustainable and resilient future.

Dedication

For Mom and Dad
Although you're gone, you still guide me every day.

Contents

List of Figures

Who Should Read This Book

I wrote this book for executives, senior leaders, and lifelong learners who want to unpack what complex business transformation really is. It's also a useful read for all the leaders who find themselves in the position of having to successfully implement a complex business transformation program. Whether you have multiple transformations under your belt or if it's your first rodeo, every transformation is different with their own singular quirks and challenges.

Foreword

Business transformation has always fascinated me—not because of the technology, the process maps, or the organizational charts but because of what it reveals about people. Every transformation, at its core, is a human story. It's about people deciding to change what they do, how they do it, and sometimes even what they believe about their work and its purpose.

That's what makes this book so important. It cuts through the noise and gives leaders a structured and practical roadmap for leading meaningful transformation. It doesn't romanticize change or reduce it to slogans. Instead, it acknowledges the reality: Transformation is complex, messy, and at times uncomfortable. But it's also where growth, innovation, and resilience are forged.

Over the past two decades as a CIO and transformation leader, I've seen firsthand how often organizations treat "transformation" as a project instead of a journey. They focus on new systems instead of new mindsets, and on timelines instead of trust. This book reminds us that successful transformation isn't about replacing one process with another—it's about aligning people, purpose, and performance around a shared future.

I especially appreciate how this book blends strategy with humanity. It recognizes that risk management, governance, and structure all matter—but so do empathy, clarity, and culture. It reminds leaders that transformation doesn't just happen to people; it must happen through them. You'll find that every chapter connects to the real world of leading teams under pressure, balancing priorities and making decisions with incomplete information. It's written for the leaders in the arena—the ones who understand that transformation is both an act of design and an act of courage.

As you read, don't just study the frameworks. Reflect on the questions they provoke. How do you want your organization to change? More importantly, how do you want it to be when the transformation is complete? The answers to those questions define not just your business but your legacy.

Blake K. Holman

CIO | Executive Coach | Leadership and Influence Strategist

Acknowledgments

I would like to recognize the many business colleagues and friends who through our interactions over the years have inspired me and contributed to my successes in life. For that I'm forever grateful. This wonderful group of people include:

Jim Bean, Pat Coffey, June Drewry, Rob Fallows, Dieter Gable, Julie Gable, Richard Goldberg, Blake Holman, Joan Holman, Andrew Jackson, Justin Jurgens, Jim Knight, Stephen Lau, Dan Leonard, Margaret Mitchell, Scot Moye, Ken Prokuski, Wally Sellman, Joel Sher, Marcus Sipolt, Jeff Stremcha, Sharon Cutcher Sykes, Mark Taylor, Mark Thomas, Peter Vogel, Patty Voight, Bill Waas

...and many others (you know who you are).

A special shout-out to *mi gente, mi familia*: Mikey, Lori, Dale, Jerry, and Susan. Your unwavering love and support mean more to me than words can ever express.

Preface

I remember when responsibility for that first complex business transformation program was dumped in my lamp. I had lots of experience working on stand-alone projects for business process reengineering, large systems implementations, and department reorganizations. However, this was a different animal—it was all those types of projects rolled into one, on a much larger scale. The business stakes were exponentially higher—as was the risk of me screwing up.

The levels of stress impacting the people involved was also noticeably greater. As the leader of the program, it was up to me to calm people down and get them focused. It was like defusing a bomb: Do I cut the red wire or the blue wire to avoid blowing everyone up?

And despite all the talk of "teamwork," my peers kept their distance, standing behind the blast wall. Some of them were afraid I would cut the wrong wire and didn't want to be collateral damage. Others would have been very happy if I cut the wrong wire. Clearly, I was going to have to figure this out on my own.

This is the book I wish I had back then.

An Overview

What Is Business Transformation?

Implementing a new technology. Reorganizing a business department. Working on a large project. Rebranding the company. These are all examples of what business transformation (BT) is NOT.

BT is the process of fundamentally altering an organization's strategy, operational models, processes, or structures. It requires a significant shift in people, processes, and technology. A successful transformation enables the business to thrive in a changing environment by increasing efficiency and resilience and creating long-term value.

Why Undertake Business Transformation?

To respond to a changing business environment:
Competitive pressures, market shifts, and new regulations are a few examples of changes in the business environment that could lead to a need to transform.

To leverage new opportunities:
Emerging technologies, global markets, and consumer trends all present new opportunities that require business transformation to allow the organization to capitalize on them.

To address economic factors impacting the business:
Business transformation may help reverse decline in performance, loss of customers, and stagnating growth.

To optimize outcomes of mergers and acquisitions:
Mergers and acquisitions often require transforming the combined processes, systems, and culture into a unified new entity.

To enable innovation:
The strategic plan may call for innovation and reinvention of the business model or product/service line.

These are explained further in Chapter 1.

When Is Business Transformation Considered Complex?

BT is classified as complex when it involves any or all these characteristics of complexity.

Innovation: If the organization is going to do something it has never done before, there is a high probability that unforeseen challenges will emerge.

Unpredictability: This refers to the extent to which there is imperfect or unknown information, thus making it difficult to predict with any certainty the future outcomes of the transformation.

Interdependencies: All transformations have many "moving parts." That in itself doesn't make the program complex. It's when individual components start affecting each other. At the start of the transformation, it's difficult to have a complete understanding of what components will have dependencies.

Technologies: When relying on technologies that are brand-new to the organization, or are not fully understood by the team, this creates significant risk.

External constraints: These are factors beyond the control of the organization. Some examples include economic shifts, geopolitical events, and regulatory changes. These can't be predicted in advance, but recognizing where an external constraint may impact the transformation effort helps with risk mitigation planning.

What Are the Components of Complex BT?

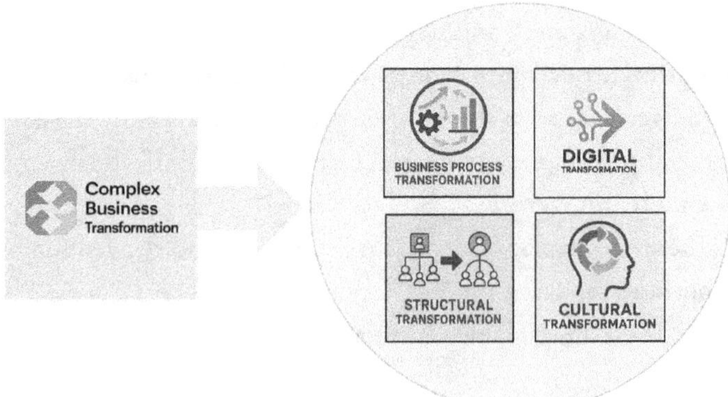

Complex business transformations involve all these subtypes of transformation:

- **Process:** Analyzing all current business processes in workflows to improve output, quality, or effectiveness.
- **Digital:** Integrating digital technologies across the business to drive fundamental change.
- **Structural:** Addresses resource composition (employee roles, staff augmentation), capabilities (functional and leadership skills and education), and allocation (right-sizing headcount, reporting lines).
- **Cultural:** Shifting the behaviors of people in support of shared goals. Assess how well employees are aligned with the organization's vision, mission, and values, and then take steps to close any gaps.

A typical business transformation initiative can be compared to remodeling a single room in your home, such as the kitchen. You build new cabinets, repaint the walls, or upgrade the appliances. Although it makes the kitchen more aesthetically pleasing and useful, the remainder of the house is substantially unaltered.

Complex business transformation, on the other hand, is like a major remodeling of the entire house. You may even decide to demolish the house and rewrite the blueprint. Rethinking the entire structure, including new technologies, making sure the house is energy-efficient, and possibly even adding more levels to allow future development are all part of the improvement process. It's a huge undertaking that impacts every facet and needs thoughtful preparation, a substantial investment of resources, and cooperation from all teams (in this example, that would be all of the contractors).

The four types of transformations are explained further in their own chapters.

How to Use This Book

This book lays the foundation for understanding what complex BT is. Practical approaches and insights for effectively leading complex BT are provided.

If you're looking for a concise overview of key concepts, read the "Top 10 Causes of Transformation Failures" and the "Summary: Best Practices to Achieve BT" in Chapter 11.

If you're looking for talking points, but not the full details, look for the "Key Insights" and "What Not to Do" summaries at the end of the chapters.

A Note About Organizational Change Management

Organizational change management (OCM) is a structured approach to help people, teams, and organizations move from where they are now to where they want to be in the future. It includes the methodologies, tools, and tactics used to handle the people side of change in order to achieve the desired business results.

The main goals are to make it easier for people to "absorb" changes, speed up the process of putting the changes into place, and make sure that the effects of change last. OCM aims to maintain productivity during transitions while also making the organization more capable of handling change in the future.

OCM is critical for large-scale initiatives that significantly impact how people do their work. That's why it must be used for complex business transformations.

Although OCM will be referenced, this book will not provide specific guidance on applying OCM. This is because OCM is a discipline in itself for which many detailed references and guides exist. If your organization doesn't already have their own OCM program, a curated list of references is provided here.

- Harvard Business Review Press, *HBR Guide to Leading Through Change*, 2024
- Ann Salerno and Lillie Brock, *The Change Cycle: How People Can Survive and Thrive in Organizational Change* (Berret-Koehler Publishers, 2008)
- John P. Kotter, *Our Iceberg is Melting* (St. Martin's Press, 2006)
- Esther Cameron and Mike Green, *Making Sense of Change Management* (Kogan Page, 2016)
- The *Change Management Institute* is dedicated to advancing the field of change management. They offer a variety of educational programs. https://change-management-institute.com/

CHAPTER 1

Assessing the Need for Transformation

The Triggers for Transformation

Changing Business Environment

Business models, operations, products, and services may need to be adjusted to respond to evolving customer needs, competitors, regulations, and economic climate. BT enables the response.

> Netflix launched as a mail-based DVD rental business in 1997. As Internet bandwidth continued to expand, they foresaw the decline in physical media and consumers switching to digital consumption. In 2007, Netflix transformed from a DVD-by-mail service to a streaming platform (Oxford Executive Institute 2024). In 2012, they extended their transformation when they began producing original content. Today, they are recognized as a leading producer of streaming content.

New Opportunities Emerge

Emerging technologies, markets, and consumer trends all present new opportunities. BT enables organizations to capitalize on them and find new purpose.

> Ecolab was a leading supplier of cleaning and maintenance products to institutional and manufacturing clients. In the early 2000s, their customers were voicing concerns about access to clean water. Recognizing water scarcity was a critical global challenge, Ecolab saw a strategic opportunity to use their chemical engineering expertise to

develop water conservation and management solutions (Anthony et al. 2019). Ecolab became a global sustainability leader for water, hygiene, and infection prevention solutions and services (Businesswire 2020).

Economic Factors

BT can help organizations reverse stagnating growth, become more cost efficient, or improve declining performance metrics (market share, revenue, etc.)

Starbucks, a specialty coffee retailer, at one point of time, had saturated the U.S. market. In order to continue growing, they had to expand into foreign markets. Their transformation approach focused on customizing market strategies, investing in digital customer engagement, while maintaining a consistent brand experience worldwide. They transformed themselves from a regional chain of coffee stores into a global lifestyle brand. In 2024, they operated over 32,000 stores in more than 80 countries (The Strategy Institute 2024).

Mergers and Acquisitions

Postmerger integration often involves a transformation of the combined business processes and systems. All postmerger integrations require a cultural transformation to set the foundation for the new combined entity.

Amazon acquired Whole Foods in 2017 to expand its footprint in physical retail and disrupt the grocery industry. The cultural contrasts between the two companies were huge. Amazon's concentration on data, centralization, and efficiency conflicted with Whole Foods' focus on decentralization and employee empowerment. Amazon imposed strict rules on how things should be done, structured processes, and performance metrics that disrupted Whole Foods' traditional way of letting employees make values-based decisions. Because Amazon failed to prioritize cultural integration in the merger, internal tensions led to a number of employees leaving. Whole Foods' identity changed within the Amazon ecosystem, which also had an impact on their customer base (Blanding 2018).

Achieving Innovation

To maintain market share, businesses in mature industries must be open to new ideas. BT can provide the first-mover advantage if the organization wants to fill a gap in the market by offering products and services that redefine expectations of their customers and give them new kinds of value.

Amazon created a cloud infrastructure to be used internally for their e-commerce platform. Through their own experience, they identified a market need for scalable, on-demand cloud computing services. They transformed their internal project into Amazon Web Services, and became a pioneer in cloud infrastructure (Colvin 2022). At the end of 2024, Amazon held a 31 percent share of the cloud computing market (Richter 2025).

Accelerating the Business Case for BT

Figure Out Whom You Must Convince

1. Start by **identifying key stakeholders.** The executive sponsor and decision makers are obvious. What is less clear are the unseen players that work behind the scenes and have significant influence (both positive and negative) over the decision makers. Ask yourself, *Who else should I include or consult with regarding this initiative?* A best practice is to develop a stakeholder map that includes all of the key players, their roles and relationships.
2. **Understand who you're dealing with.** Run through the following questions as you review your stakeholder map.
    - Who is most likely to be an ally?
    - Who are the detractors, and how much power do they have?

- What are the "hot buttons" for each of the key stakeholders?
- Do I have the relationship capital to influence those in authority?

Remember, in every situation there will be natural conflicts and alliances based on the interests of the people involved. These conflicts will vary depending on the subject. You may have had a close relationship with an executive yesterday, but a new topic may emerge that will put you at odds with that same person.

You may run into a situation where you know who you must convince, but presenting a business case to them isn't the right approach. You may have to figure out how to position it as their idea and then help them think through the case for it.

Understanding the political landscape is important as you prepare to state your case for BT. Ensure that the business case addresses as many of the stakeholder concerns as possible. Be ready to speak to all of them. Political implications may also depend on where you sit in the organization's hierarchy (e.g., you report to someone who happens to be out of favor with decision makers) or where you are geographically located (e.g. you work for a global company, but you don't sit at headquarters).

Present the Case for Making the Investment

1. **Show how BT supports the business strategy**

   Explain the "Why" to your audience. Demonstrate how BT supports the strategic goals of the organization (e.g., growth, innovation, improved customer experience, sustainability).

   Focus on the competitive pressures facing the organization, including new competitors in your vertical, shifting consumer expectations, and regulatory changes.

   Finally, state what will happen if the organization does not transform. Consequences could include loss of market share due to inability to meet consumer demands; product pricing increases due to outdated processes; potential for disruption due to a technology "burning platform."

   The objective is to motivate the decision makers to act quickly and decisively.

2. **Define the objectives and scope of BT**
   Create a compelling and inspiring vision of *what* BT will achieve. Frame the goals of BT based on alignment to the business strategy. For example, if the strategy is to expand into new markets, the BT goals must visibly support that.

   Identify the functional areas that will be impacted by transformation. For complex BT initiatives, it will involve transformation of business processes, organizational structure, technology, and culture.

   The executive team will want confirmation that BT is in line with the organization's vision and mission. Paint a clear picture for them.
3. **Quantify the benefits of BT**
   Begin with identifying and quantifying the financial benefits. Successful BT can reduce costs through process optimization and automation, improving legacy infrastructure, and leveraging technology to improve operational efficiency. BT can also improve revenue growth by improving customer retention through personalization, providing faster time to market for products and services. The financial benefits must be expressed in concrete terms, such as projected cost reduction or savings, and productivity improvement metrics. Be clear on how the investment in BT impacts both top and bottom lines.

   Don't forget to address the qualitative benefits. These are harder to affix a dollar amount to but still represent strategic value. Examples of these are higher employee engagement, increased customer satisfaction, cybersecurity resilience. Where possible, these should be linked to measurable indicators, e.g., employee retention rates are one indicator of employee engagement.

   Because most BT initiatives can be lengthy, your benefits discussion should balance short-term wins with long-term value creation. Talk about early milestones—such as reduced cycle times or lower maintenance costs. An initiative that demonstrates incremental progress over time will be viewed more favorably. In the long run, stress the deeper benefits of BT. Examples are building a culture of innovation, the ability to be agile in response to market or regulatory change.

4. **Assess the risks and develop a mitigation plan**
Complex BT involves significant changes to strategy, operations, technology, and culture. Effective risk management is a key enabler of BT. Integrating risk management into the transformation journey ensures that the strategic goals are met with control and accountability. Chapter 7 elaborates on risk management for BT.
5. **Explain the investment rationale**
To secure executive support and ultimately approval to proceed, the investment case must present a compelling view of the value created for the organization. Indicate everything that the investment will cover so that the executives will understand the scale and scope of commitment you're asking them to make. They need to understand that BT is accomplished over phases that require an initial outlay of funding and continuing operational investment.

    The business case must reframe the costs into a value proposition. Refer back to the quantitative financial benefits that you identified and remind them of the qualitative benefits as well.

    Executives will expect you to have done a thorough ROI (return on investment) analysis with realistic assumptions about timelines, adoption rates and market impact. Boost your credibility by presenting a balanced payback period, total cost of ownership and the ongoing benefits the organization can gain from BT.

    Finally, incorporate the results of your risk analysis. The decision makers will want to understand the potential pitfalls and how you've addressed mitigating them. You want to reassure them that the proposed investment in BT is disciplined, controlled and in line with the organization's risk appetite.
6. **Explain your governance approach**
Successful BT requires strong governance and metrics. Governance provides the structure for decision making, accountability, and oversight. It ensures that the transformation activities remain aligned with the business strategy and that the identified risks are managed. Chapter 8 explains the governance approach that should be in place to ensure the success of BT.

    Establishing a comprehensive measurement system for financial and nonfinancial results is crucial. Key performance indicators

(KPIs) show progress and impact. Regular review of metrics allows leaders to track benefits realization, provide early detection of transformation issues, and adjust BT strategies quickly. Suggested metrics are provided in the chapters relating to the components of BT.

The narrative should frame BT as a way to help the business accomplish its strategy—that it's not just another IT project or reengineering of a business process. It should explain how BT makes the business more competitive, resilient and strengthens the customer experience. Emphasize risk, return, and strategic alignment. Demonstrate that this is a disciplined investment with credible benefits. Don't forget to include the human factors. Point out how BT can empower employees, encourage innovation, and require strong leadership to guide the necessary change in culture.

Key Insights

- BT involves a wholesale rethinking and restructuring of how a business operates. If you're only considering incremental improvements, you don't have a need for transformation.
- Build a coalition of support with key stakeholders before presenting the formal proposal.

What Not to Do

- Fail to connect BT to the organization's overall business strategy.
- Emphasize technical details over business outcomes.
- Present a flawed or incomplete business case.

CHAPTER 2

Planning the BT Implementation

Fans of the "Big Bang Theory" will remember when Sheldon and Leonard played Tri Dimensional (3D) Chess.

To play chess well, you need the ability to visualize, memorize moves, understand patterns, apply logic, think ahead, make informed decisions under pressure, and accept the consequences of your actions. 3D Chess takes all of these to another level.

Executing complex BT is very much like playing 3D Chess.

The rules as you know them don't always apply. A higher level of complexity is involved as you have multiple layers of transformation activities to coordinate simultaneously. It isn't sufficient to think on a single plane; now you must anticipate how each action will have a ripple effect across multiple dimensions.

Here's a suggested game plan.

Establish Change Sequencing and Dependencies

For each stream of transformation (business process, digital, structural) list the major milestones. Then look at the critical interdependencies between those milestones. Some things to consider:

- Do new technologies enable the process changes, or do the business processes need to change first?
- Are reorganizations needed to support new processes, or do they create the capacity for technology adoption?
- Which changes are prerequisites for others?

Create a master timeline that sequences these changes. Now look at your master list through your cultural lens. As the leader of BT, some questions to ask yourself:

- Can I clearly explain *why* this change is necessary—beyond saving money or being more efficient?
- Who will be the most impacted and how will their day-to-day work change?
- For people who feel like they're losing something in this change, how can I best support them?
- What's the capacity for people to take on this transformation challenge?
- Am I doing enough to allow the organization to realize sustained benefits from transformation?
- Am I practicing empathetic and resilient leadership, so the team feels safe to follow?

Create Integrated Workstreams

Instead of planning activities for the individual streams, structure the workstreams around *business outcomes*. You would combine the changes for applicable business processes, technology, and structures. For example:

- Customer Experience workstream
- Operational Efficiency workstream
- Employee Engagement workstream
- Investor Relations workstream

This approach ensures changes work together cohesively.

Design Transition States

A risky period in transformation is when you're partially through the transformation. This is where issues due to disconnected activities will surface with a vengeance, and employees are feeling the effects of "change fatigue." No wonder it's referred to as the "messy middle." Plan specific transition states where people know:

- Which processes to follow during the change period
- How to escalate issues when systems are in conflict
- Who has authority when reporting structures are in flux
- How to get support for new technology solutions

Keep in mind the human element and that people are often motivated to change by "what's in it for me" (WIIFM). How people are treated in the change process will make a huge difference. Ensure that you have support structures in place that provide timely responses.

Build Change Capability Within the Organization

Recruit Change Agents who are dedicated to the BT initiative. They will be the ambassadors that advocate and champion the change activities. They'll model the behaviors that the organization needs to be successful with BT.

Don't forget to develop middle managers specifically on how to lead through ambiguity. They'll be fielding most of the questions from front-line staff that are navigating the multiple changes.

Explain the Big Picture, Multiple Times

Communicate about BT holistically to help people understand the larger strategic vision. When people see the bigger picture, they're more willing to tolerate temporary ambiguity and having to do some extra work.

There's a common saying that "repetition is the mother of learning." Repetition helps reduce cognitive load, making complex ideas easier for people to process over time (Matuntuta 2025). Talk about the big picture consistently and often.

Define What Success Looks Like

This is easier said than done, yet it is the most important task you must complete to set up the BT initiative for success.

The Challenges of Defining Success

Complex BT is a large initiative consisting of interdependent components. This presents a basic tension: individual components can succeed while the overall initiative fails, and what is best for one part frequently harms another. For example, business processes may have been successfully transformed, but it disrupts the company's structure and culture. It's natural for teams to prioritize their own deliverables over the interfaces and interactions between components. This can cause each team to optimize their own component in ways that hurt the initiative as a whole. People don't always understand the interdependencies well at first: Sequencing assumptions turn out to be wrong, and unexpected behaviors from component interactions can't be predicted. Additionally, the complexity of BT makes it hard to hold people accountable because everyone insists their part works fine, even if the whole effort is struggling. At this stage, there is a danger that governance mechanisms become performative rather than truly assuring alignment.

The measurement challenges exacerbate these systemic issues. Success criteria tend to favor what is easily measured for individual components over important system-level outcomes. Different stakeholders define success via opposing lenses: short-term victories versus long-term capability, technical functionality versus business value, delivery speed versus quality. These tensions compound across all components and interactions.

It's hard to maintain a shared understanding of success when you're working with many teams. This requires enormous communication effort. If you can't maintain a cohesive vision across all teams, they will end up working toward incompatible goals without realizing it until integration.

All of these combined can lead to success definitions that are both too vague to be useful and too rigid to accommodate the unavoidable surprises that complexity brings.

Take a Structured Approach

Follow a process that involves defining, aligning, and validating goals, outcomes, and metrics.

1. Define the time horizons
   - Don't wait until the end of the initiative to measure your success. Based on your BT plan, decide logical assessment stages.
   - Distinguish between early wins, mid-term milestones, and long-term outcomes.
   - Consider both the completion of BT and the sustained impact it's supposed to have.
2. Clarify the purpose of BT
   - Why was the BT initiative launched?
   - Clarify the business problems being addressed.
   - What were the outcomes cited in the business case?
   - Ensure alignment with the broader company strategy.
3. Engage the key stakeholders to understand their perspectives of success
   - What does each group or individual see as valuable progress?
   - Are they purpose driven or outcomes driven?

     (If you are purpose driven, you prioritize values, mission, and long-term impact. Success to you must be aligned with core beliefs. If you are outcomes driven, you focus on measurable results, performance metrics, and short-term achievements. As a leader of complex BT, you will be faced with balancing both perspectives.)
4. Define quantitative metrics

   For example:
   - Financial metrics (profitability, ROI, etc.)
   - Operational metrics (efficiency gains, time to market, etc.)
   - Customer metrics (retention, NPS [Net Promoter Score®], etc.)
   - Market metrics (market share, capitalization, etc.)
5. Define qualitative metrics, for example:
   - Behavior changes
   - Improved collaboration
   - Enhanced knowledge
   - Stronger stakeholder relationships
   - Brand improvement
6. Create graduated definitions of success
   - Minimum viable success: What must happen for BT not to be considered a failure?

    - Expected success: What does a solid, successful outcome look like?
    - Exceptional success: What would exceed expectations?
7. Identify what success is NOT
    - What outcomes do you want to actively avoid?
    - What trade-offs are unacceptable?
    - What constraints must you respect?
8. Document your findings
    - List all success metrics with established baselines, targets, and timeframes.
    - The targets should be ambitious yet achievable.
    - Assign owners to each metric.
    - Define how and when each will be measured.
9. Validate the success metrics with stakeholders
    - Gain alignment across all stakeholders.
    - Get explicit commitment for ownership.
10. Plan for ongoing review and adaptation
    - Schedule periodic reassessments of success criteria.
    - When and how will you update the definition of success if conditions change?
    - Create feedback loops to ensure continuous alignment.
    - Plan retrospectives at key milestones to gather learnings.

Leonard doesn't play 3D chess very well. Sheldon tells him, "It must be humbling to suck at so many different levels." Complex BT can be humbling, but taking a detailed, logical approach to planning and having that vision of success up front will make it less daunting.

CHAPTER 3

Business Process Transformation

Figure 3.1 Logo of BT

While BT addresses broader goals, business process transformation (BPT) focuses on the incremental changes required to attain them. Without successful BPT, you'll have ineffective BT. In turn, BPT initiatives may necessitate broader organizational changes to accommodate changed procedures (refer to Chapter 5, Structural Transformation).

Approach to Revising Business Processes for BT

Taking a systematic approach to BPT ensures that changes are made based on clear goals and data, not on gut feelings or politics. This helps get people on board and monitor the success of the changes.

1. **Validate transformation goals**
   Clarify the broader objectives of BT, verifying that the goals remain aligned with the organization's vision.
2. **Identify the processes to be transformed**
   Identify the processes that are pertinent to the BT initiative. Prioritize processes based on the organization's strategy.
3. **Analyze the current process**
   Look for areas of improvement (e.g., inefficiencies, processes that are outdated) and potential roadblocks (e.g., the process is no longer aligned with the organization's goals). Decompose the current process into component tasks to identify issues to address.
4. **Engage stakeholders**
   Meet with key stakeholders to discuss the processes impacted by BT. Their input is important for the redesigning of the processes. Incorporate organizational change management (OCM) to address resistance and keep all stakeholders aligned.
5. **Leverage Data Analytics**
   Use data analytics to assess process performance. Cycle times, transaction costs, and others provide the quantitative basis for process improvement. Qualitative insights (e.g., customer satisfaction feedback) should also be considered along with the data-driven findings.
6. **Design the new process**
   Based on the analytics, design the new process. This could involve simplifying and standardizing work, automating repetitive tasks, and eliminating low-value work.
7. **Align processes with BT Goals**
   Ensure that the redesigned processes directly support the overarching transformation objectives.
8. **Start with pilot testing**
   It's recommended that implementation of the new process starts with small-scale pilots within a controlled environment. This provides an opportunity to gather user feedback and identify issues so they can be addressed before a full-scale implementation.
9. **Implement and monitor**
   Deploy the new processes organizationwide and monitor the performance of the new process in production to ensure they are working as intended and are meeting the expected performance metrics.

10. **Practice continuous improvement**
BPT very often isn't a one and done exercise. After the initial successes, and after the "settling in" period, you may realize that the new processes were not quite complete and need to continue to change. Make allowances in your program for continuous improvement of the processes, metrics, analytics, and so on.

BPT Profile: IKEA

Founded in Sweden in 1943, IKEA today is the world's largest home furnishing retailer with more than 400 stores in 50 countries.

From the start, the in-store experience provided to customers distinguished IKEA from competitor furniture retailers. In 2018, they recognized the growing demand for online shopping and made the strategic decision to pivot to e-commerce (Hensel 2020).

This necessitated the reengineering of its **order fulfillment and logistics operations** (Stackpole 2021). IKEA's stores were designed primarily for in-person shopping, with customers picking up items themselves. Under the new e-commerce model, IKEA needed to adapt its business processes to handle online orders as well. Some of the key business process changes made:

1. IKEA restructured its physical stores to double as **fulfillment centers for online orders**. This required changes in inventory management, storage layouts, and workflows to accommodate both in-store shoppers and online order processing.
2. Algorithms were implemented to **optimize the supply chain**. To maintain client satisfaction, it was critical to determine the most efficient source for fulfilling an order—whether from a store or a distribution center. This shift streamlined delivery times and reduced costs.
3. IKEA introduced "Click & Collect," allowing customers to order online and pick up their items at a nearby store. This required reengineering processes to ensure seamless coordination between online systems and in-store operations.
4. Where physical stores operate under traditional business hours, e-commerce operates around the clock. IKEA had to adapt its logistics and staffing to meet the demands of a **24/7 online marketplace.**

Measuring Progress

The core of BT is operational excellence. Metrics for BT should highlight improvement of inefficiencies, track process adaptability, and reflect improvements in speed, quality, and value delivery. Metrics should be comparative over time, sensitive to change, and relevant to stakeholder expectations.

Strategic Alignment

Metric	Purpose	Suggested approach
Profitability Impact	Assess whether process improvements are making the anticipated contributions to the bottom line.	• Isolate the profit directly attributable to the process changes by comparing scenarios with and without it • Look at revenue uplift (new revenue streams, increased sales, or market share gains tied to BPT)
Time to Market	Measure how quickly new products and services are launched	• Average number of days from concept to launch

Process Performance

Metric	Purpose	Suggested approach
Cycle time reduction	Assesses speed and efficiency	[(Baseline time − Current time) / Baseline time] × 100
Error rates	Indicates quality issues or inefficiencies requiring rework	(Number of defects) / (Total transactions)] × 100

Adoption and Engagement

Metric	Purpose	Suggested approach
Training Completion	Tracks readiness of employees to perform under the new processes	% staff who completed training and passed a postassessment
Process Compliance	How consistently users are following the new process	(Number of compliant transactions) / (Total transactions) × 100
User Adoption rate	The number of intended users actively using the new processes	(Number of active users) / (Total target users) × 100

Key Insights

- **Make sure BPT directly supports the strategic direction of the organization**
  Misalignment can lead to wasted resources, disconnected changes, siloed behavior by departments—all having a negative impact on the bottom line. For example, ACME Corporation's strategy is to differentiate itself through superb personalized customer experience. However, in a move that is not supportive of the strategy, the operations team decides to implement a chatbot that reduces 90 percent of customer interactions with humans, and they subsequently downsize their call center staff. This results in a spike in complaints because the chatbot cannot gauge the emotional context of customer interactions. Brand reputation suffers as angry customers make negative posts on social media. ACME loses customers and sales revenue drops.
- **Understand the current state before designing the future state**
  Many organizations rush to introduce new processes based on best practices or vendor suggestions without first mapping out their existing workflows. This results in solutions that do not address actual pain points or introduce unexpected issues. Effective transformation starts with rigorous process mapping, identifying bottlenecks, assessing current performance metrics, and determining why processes have evolved to their current condition. This foundational knowledge ensures that the new process design addresses actual challenges rather than theoretical ones.
- **Focus on end-to-end value, not just local optimization**
  Improving select processes in isolation often results in problems in other parts of the organization. For example, streamlining order processing can make the workload overwhelming for the fulfillment team. We've seen in the ACME example that automating customer service negatively impacted

satisfaction scores. Successful BPT takes into account how processes connect across departments, systems, and customer touchpoints. This systems thinking approach ensures that process changes really do improve the overall performance of the business instead of merely shifting problems to different areas.

What Not To Do

- ✗ **Treat BPT as another incremental change initiative**
  BPT is meant to fundamentally rethink and reshape how work gets done, not just minor tweaks. The biggest mistake you can make is approaching BPT with the mindset of, "How can we make this current process better?" instead of, "If we're starting from scratch, how do we design this to get the results we want?" In addition, don't let existing department boundaries, job roles, or reporting structures limit your thinking. This is the time to challenge all legacy assumptions and constraints.
- ✗ **Overlook cross-functional dependencies**
  When you focus too narrowly, BPT is likely to fail. For example, improving processes in one department without redesigning the end-to-end value chain. This leads to delays, misalignment, and conflicting goals.
- ✗ **Underestimate the cultural and organizational impact**
  BPT fundamentally changes how people work. Jobs are eliminated or combined; people have to learn new skills. A lot of effort goes into the technical and process design aspects of transformation, but the cultural implications are often neglected. If you don't deal with the human and cultural issues, people will resist. They'll find methods to get around the new processes and eventually revert to the old way of doing things.

CHAPTER 4

Digital Transformation

Figure 4.1 Digital transformation

The term "digital transformation" ("DX") implies that it is all about technology, or something digital that you can buy or outsource.

A more accurate definition of DX is "the use of technology to radically improve performance or reach of enterprises" (Westerman et al. 2014).

When undertaking digital transformation, always follow the tenet "form follows function."

It's critical to first understand the problem from a business perspective. Technology-centered discussions should always come last. A recommended approach to DX is as follows:

Assess the Current Level of Digital Maturity

Evaluate the existing digital capabilities and technology infrastructure.

1. **Audit the current technology stack**
   Inventory all the hardware, software, cloud services, and integrations that are currently in use. Make a map of how systems depend on each other and look for overlaps or holes. Add information about the version, the cost of the license, and the timeline for maintenance. Be sure to include components that often go undetected or are overlooked: custom applications, integrations, manual data exports, transformations, and import elements, among others.
2. **Assess data management practices and analytics capabilities**
   Look at how data moves through your organization, from acquiring and storing it to processing it and creating reports. Audit the quality of the data, the rules for using it, the backup plans, and the analytics tools you already have. Discover new methods to leverage data and improve decision making.
3. **Conduct a digital skills inventory**
   Assess the existing digital skills of the employees. Look at past and present experience, and qualifications.
4. **Document the current state of IT governance**
   Look at the current rules, policies, and ways of making decisions about managing and investing in technology. Document the workflows for approving documents, the process by which budgets are allocated, how IT fits in with business goals.
5. **Document the current state of data governance**
   Get a clear overview of how data is maintained, safeguarded, and used within the organization. This includes establishing the governance scope, roles, and operating model; assessing standards for data quality, metadata, and life cycle management; understanding data security, privacy, and compliance processes; inventorying existing policies, tools, and technologies; and identifying current challenges or gaps. The objective is to provide a structured baseline that will inform your strategic data decisions, for DX.
6. **Identify technical debt and constraints of legacy systems**
   Inventory older systems that might slow down your ability to be flexible or productive. Look at the expenses of maintenance, the risks of security holes, the difficulties of integration, and the business risk of system failures.

7. **Evaluate the cybersecurity posture and compliance readiness**
   Assess if present security measures, incident response protocols, and compliance with relevant regulations are up to date. Find the vulnerabilities in your security posture.
8. **Document the current digital customer experience**
   Map the entire customer journey across all digital touchpoints. Look at how users engage with your site, how many people convert to being customers, and what problems they're experiencing. Utilize customer feedback to lend relevance to the documented experience at the point in time of your analysis.

Develop the Future State Objectives

1. **New digital objectives must align with the overall business strategy before defining the DX goals**
   Gain a full understanding of your organization's long-term goals, strategic priorities, and competitive position. Link digital projects to company goals (e.g., improve customer retention, market expansion, and so on). Ensure that every digital investment helps you reach the bigger strategic goals instead of pursuing technology for its own sake.
2. **Describe in detail the customer experience, post-DX**
   Envision the best possible customer experience at all points of contact. Describe how customers will learn about, evaluate, purchase, and use your goods and services. Think about the level of customer support you need to provide across all possible channels. Think inclusively to accommodate customers who are digital natives and those who need a mix of digital and physical experiences.
3. **Identify new revenue opportunities**
   Find out how digital tools can lead to new revenue streams. Think about direct revenue models, and indirect benefits (e.g., improved customer lifetime value). Also evaluate if data and analytics can be leveraged to generate new revenue. For example, a manufacturing company can embed Internet of Things (IoT) sensors into their equipment, collect real-time performance data, and apply analytics to predict maintenance schedules and optimize energy efficiency.

This data-driven insight lets the company launch subscription-based offerings, such as proactive support plans, that deliver value to customers while generating recurring income.

4. **Establish targets for operational efficiencies**
   Set specific goals for process automation, cost reduction, and resource optimization.
5. **Identify the organizational skills and structure required for successful DX**
   Compare the required skills for the future against the skills inventory that you compiled when assessing the current state and quantify the gaps. This will help you understand the skills that need to be developed or acquired.

   You'll also need to think about the roles and structures required to support DX into the future. This may include identifying new positions, changing the job specifications for current roles, establishing cross-functional teams and thinking about the best way to manage digital projects.
6. **Establish a data strategy and analytics objectives**
   Data governance is key for the organization to make the best use of the data. Identify how the organization will consider data as a strategic asset, from collection and storage to analysis and action.
7. **Define the target technology architecture**
   Design the future state technology stack. Don't simply fix current problems; also think about flexibility, interoperability, and how best to position the organization to easily adapt to changing business needs. The technology architecture must be designed such that it can easily accommodate ongoing improvements.

Design the Proposed Solution

1. Study the technology available in the market that will best achieve the DX goals
   - **Research the technology landscape:** Stay up to date with both emerging and established technologies. Some areas that may apply to your organization include, but are not limited to: cloud platforms, AI/ML (artificial intelligence/machine learning), data

analytics platforms, customer experience technologies, and integration solutions.

- **Map solutions to DX Goals:** Create a matrix that shows how different technologies can help you achieve DX goals. For each goal, figure out which technological solutions could help reach it, and how they fit with what you want to accomplish.
- **Analyze the vendor ecosystem:** Research the best providers in each technology category that meets your needs. Evaluate their market position, product roadmaps, financial stability, partnership ecosystems, and customer satisfaction ratings. Include both established players and new start-ups that might offer competitive advantages.
- **Assess technology maturity:** Evaluate the maturity level of a range of technologies, from cutting-edge products to tried-and-true business solutions. Weigh the possible benefits of new technologies against the implementation risks and the organization's readiness to adopt them.
- **Cost–benefit analysis:** Understand TCO (total cost of ownership) for the technologies selected. TCO includes licensing, implementation, training, ongoing maintenance and support, and decommissioning costs. Compare this to the expected benefits and ROI timelines. Think about both strategic value creation and the quantitative returns.
- **Review integration and compatibility:** Check how well the new technology solutions work with your current systems and future architecture. Consider API availability, data portability, security compatibility, and how difficult it will be to set up in your current environment.
- **Make sure the tech impacts will last:** Look at how well each technology can grow with your organization and change to meet new business needs. Think about vendor roadmaps, how technology changes over time, and the chance that technology will become outdated.
- **Plan for pilots and proof-of-concept planning:** Identify technologies that warrant need more study through pilot programs or proof of concepts. Make sure your testing and assessment

criteria match your success metrics and the time frame for putting them into action.

2. Develop a comprehensive **solutions architecture** that bridges current state to future objectives
   This may include any or all of the following components:
   - **Business architecture**: maps the business capabilities to the solution.
   - **Information architecture:** displays how information must be organized from the user perspective.
   - **Information Security architecture**: a framework that defines how the organization will protect information from cyberthreats.
   - **System architecture:** shows how the different parts of a computer system work together.
   - **Application architecture:** the blueprint for how different software applications are structured and work together.
   - **Technical architecture:** a design that outlines how different technology components (e.g., servers, databases, networks) fit together and interact.

DX Profile: IKEA

In the previous chapter, the business process transformation that IKEA pursued as part of their pivot to e-commerce was discussed. IKEA's new strategy also involved digital transformation. IKEA leveraged several cutting-edge technologies to modernize their operations and enhance the customer experience.

1. IKEA had always made effective use of staging furniture in their physical stores. In the move to e-commerce, they had to bridge the gap between the physical shopping experience that customers had come to expect, and online shopping. **Augmented reality (AR)** was deployed to allow customers to visualize furniture in their homes before purchasing.
2. Logistics improvements, inventory management, and personalized product recommendations were powered by **AI algorithms**.

3. IKEA introduced **autonomous drones** for inventory management in warehouses. These drones efficiently count stock and monitor inventory across multiple locations.
4. **Data analytics** were embedded into its decision-making processes, enabling better forecasting, supply chain optimization, and customer insights.
5. IKEA made a strategic decision to **partner with other third-party e-commerce platforms** to expand its digital reach.

IKEA's complex business transformation saw their e-commerce sales triple within three years, and strengthened their global market position (Stackpole 2021).

Measuring Progress

DX metrics should not only track adoption of the technology but also cultural shift, customer impact, agility, and long-term value creation. They should be consistently trackable over time, and responsive to evolving business priorities. Here are a few suggested metrics for tracking DX progress.

Metric	Purpose	Suggested approach
Digital Business Profitability	Measure the bottom-line impact and business value generated from DX	• Percentage of revenue from digital channels, or digitally enabled products • Revenue per customer, digital versus traditional channels • Cost savings from process automation • Time-to-market improvements for new products and services
Employee Productivity Improvement	How effectively employees are embracing and applying new digital tools and processes	• Track training participation • Adoption rates across digital tools and platforms • Time to completion of tasks, pre- and postimplementation of technology • Employee surveys to understand perceived ease of use and satisfaction

Metric	Purpose	Suggested approach
Customer Experience	Understand how DX is impacting your customers	• Customer digital engagement (e.g., app usage, digital transaction volume) • Sentiment analysis on interactions • Customer lifetime value improvements from digital touchpoints
Technical Debt Reduction	Monitor progress in modernizing legacy systems and reducing complexity	• Developer surveys to assess perceived debt • Tools such as McKinsey's Technical Debt Scorer (TDS) (Blumberg et al. 2022)

Key Insights

- **Build security and infrastructure readiness**
  DX security and infrastructure readiness means that an organization can protect its data, systems and operations while also using new technologies. It means having a strong, flexible IT infrastructure that can handle cloud migration, real-time analytics, and evolving cybersecurity threats without affecting performance or compliance. When infrastructure is obsolete or fragmented, DX actions fail, and vulnerabilities proliferate. Readiness isn't just about technology; it's also about strategy. It includes making sure that IT and business goals are in sync, having proactive governance, and a culture that values resilience and agility.
- **Data strategy and governance**
  Data is what makes things like analytics, AI, and tailored customer experiences possible. Before you start pursuing DX, establish strong data governance processes, make sure that the data are of high quality and easy to access across systems, and understand how to extract relevant information from it. You will need to implement proper security and privacy controls, as well as the analytical tools needed to make data-driven

decisions. Digital projects can't achieve their full potential without data that is clean, integrated, and well governed.

- **Technology infrastructure and architecture**
  For DX to succeed, it needs a robust and scalable technology foundation. Evaluate your existing IT infrastructure and update legacy systems that can't handle new digital features. The technology architecture should be flexible, not just stable. It should allow for quick testing, quick deployment of new features, and the capacity to scale as needed. As you attempt to build digital solutions on top of rigid, outdated infrastructure that becomes an obstacle rather than an enabler of DX.

What Not To Do

- **Treat DX as another technology project**
  It's a common mistake to delegate all the responsibility for DX to the IT team. DX is a business strategy to accomplish organizational goals. Leaving everything to IT may result in a final solution that is technically sound but fails to deliver the required business value.
- **Take a technology-first approach**
  Don't get caught up in adopting new technology without fully understanding how they solve specific business problems or add value. This leads to costly technology implementations that don't improve outcomes and may even increase complexity. Instead, start with a business first assessment. Get the answer to: "What is the business problem we must solve?" *before* going down the path of digital tool selection.

CHAPTER 5

Structural Transformation

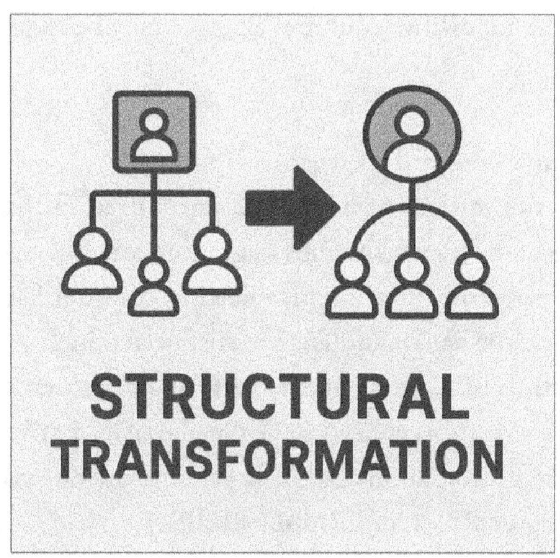

Figure 5.1 Logo of ST

Structural transformation (ST) in the context of BT refers to a fundamental reorganization of the organization's internal framework (how it is organized, governed, and how work flows) to achieve its strategic goals.

Triggers for ST

Organizations usually need to adjust their structure when big shifts occur in the internal or external environment that make the current structure ineffective or misaligned with goals.

The key is knowing when your structure is getting in the way of achieving your strategic objectives.

1. The business strategy requires an organization designed for the future.
2. The benefits from an M&A (mergers and acquisitions) transaction should be realized.

3. Customer needs have shifted.
4. Business performance is lower than expected.
5. Operational inefficiencies are evident.
6. Employees' skill sets are misaligned with their functions.

Key Structural Aspects

Any or all of the following structural changes may be required to accomplish BT goals.

1. **Reconfiguration of the Organization**
   Design organizational structures that may need to change: job roles, reporting lines, team structures (e.g., functional to matrix).
   A multilayered organization may need to consider flattening hierarchies to achieve agility and faster decision making.
2. **Introduction of New Business Units or Functions**
   New departments may need to be created. Alternatively, groups may be merged or eliminated to streamline operations.
3. **Redefining of Roles and Responsibilities**
   Accountabilities may shift to align with new business models. Cross-functional teams may be leveraged for better collaboration and responsiveness.
4. **Leadership and Governance Adjustments**
   The organization may need to establish new governance entities. Leadership styles may need to adapt to new cultural norms (e.g., collaborative, innovative, customer-centric).
5. **Integrating or Separating Activities**
   Decision making may move to being decentralized from centralized, or vice versa. In cases of mergers and acquisitions, departments could be merged post-acquisition, or business units carved out for spinoffs.
6. **New Operating Models**
   Transformation may require moving from traditional models to platform-based, hybrid, or ecosystem-driven models. Emphasis could shift to agile or lean operations away from traditional rigid structures.

Approaching Structural Transformation

A thorough strategy that considers both the human and technical sides of change is essential. Here's the best way to approach it.

Start with Strategic Alignment

Before restructuring anything, make sure the proposed structural changes are directly linked to the BT objectives. Determine whether current organizational structures help or hinder the desired future state. This clarity precludes restructuring for its own sake and helps you to make targeted changes to achieve your objectives.

Design for Efficiency and Adaptability

Modern organizational structures must strike a balance between operational efficiency and the ability to adapt. Consider hybrid models that combine functional expertise with cross-functional teams, or matrix designs that facilitate both vertical accountability and horizontal cooperation. The objective is to build structures that can adapt as your transformation develops, rather than requiring major overhauls.

Sequence Changes Thoughtfully

Don't attempt to restructure everything at once. Prioritize changes based on their impact to the BT goals and the organization's capacity for change. Begin with the areas where structural improvements will have the greatest immediate positive impact on employee experience and business performance. Then build momentum from that for more complex changes.

Address the Shift in Power Dynamics

Changes to the structure of an organization will always change who has power and influence. Identify the key stakeholders who might be affected and get them involved early on. Be open about how roles, responsibilities, and reporting lines will change, and provide clear rationale for these decisions.

Invest in Capability Building

Structure follows strategy, but so does capability. As you change the way the organization is set up, allocate resources to help employees get the skills and knowledge they need to succeed in the new environment. This could include learning new leadership skills, new methods to work together, or the technical skills needed for new jobs.

Reinforce and Optimize

Create feedback mechanisms to determine whether structural changes are achieving the desired results. This includes both quantitative measurements for performance and qualitative measures for employee engagement and organizational health. Prepare to make course corrections based on what you discover.

Structural Transformation Profile: Airbnb

Airbnb is a global online marketplace that connects people looking to rent out their homes with those seeking accommodation. It was founded in 2008 and is headquartered in San Francisco, CA.

At the start of the COVID-19 pandemic, Airbnb's bookings dropped by over 70 percent, and its private valuation dropped from $31 billion to around $18 billion (de Leon 2022). The company suddenly found itself in survival mode.

Airbnb's CEO Brian Chesky declared "Travel as we knew it was over" (Yohn 2020). The company responded to the crisis by undertaking a complex business transformation. The structural transformation component included the following actions:

- Reduced its workforce by 25 percent (ca. 1,900 employees) (de Leon 2022)
- Internally, Airbnb restructured into smaller, more agile teams that focused on business functions such as Trust and Safety, Guest Experience, and Hosting. This matrix-style model facilitated

faster decision making and improved alignment with changing customer needs (Yohn 2020).

- Airbnb decided to include hosts (the people who own the properties) in the scope of the definition of "Airbnb Team," considering them as much a part of Airbnb as the employees. Early on, $250 million was allocated to reimburse hosts for canceled stays. A $10 million fund was created to help them pay for their mortgages (Yohn 2020).

Measuring Progress

Apply ST metrics to track both the changes that are made to the structure and how they impact organizational effectiveness. Because structure affects how people work, make decisions, and collaborate, your assessment should blend **quantitative metrics** with **qualitative indicators** across a range of areas.

Organizational Design

Metric	Purpose	Suggested approach
Reporting relationships and hierarchy	Assess whether streamlined reporting lines are improving decision making speed and accountability	• Look at changes in organizational charts, span of control, and layers of management • Track reductions or increases in hierarchies • Measure speed of decision making at various levels of the organization
Role clarity and accountability	Ensure employees understand their new responsibilities and can do their jobs well within the transformed structure	• Survey employees on understanding of their roles and responsibilities • See if there are gaps in accountability, or overlapping roles
Cross-functional integration	Confirm that structural changes are breaking down silos and enabling collaboration to achieve strategic goals	• Frequency of communication between departments that were previously siloed • Number of cross-departmental initiatives

Decision Making

Metric	Purpose	Suggested approach
Allocation of decision rights	Validate that decision-making authority is positioned at the right levels of the organization to improve speed and quality of strategic and operational decisions	• Are decisions centralized or decentralized • Track speed of decision making and correlate to the quality of outcomes • Percentage of decisions that are made at the appropriate organization level
Committee and meeting effectiveness	Ensure that these governance structures add value rather than create bureaucracy	• Frequency and duration of meetings compared to outcomes • Track the contribution of these governance structures to achieving the strategy
Information flow patterns	Confirm that critical information reaches decision makers quickly and accurately	• The frequency of information sharing • The speed at which critical information gets to the decision makers

Workflow and Process

Metric	Purpose	Suggested approach
Process efficiency	Demonstrate that structural changes eliminate inefficiencies and enable higher quality work output	• Cycle times • Number of hand-offs between departments • Elimination of redundant tasks
Resource allocation effectiveness	Verify that the new structure is optimizing resource utilization and directing them toward strategic priorities	• Monitor how resources (people, budget, technology) are distributed across the new structure • Look at utilization rates
Agility and responsiveness	Measure whether the structural changes enable the organization to adapt quickly to market changes and customer needs	• Track time to market • Response time to address customer needs • Agility of the new structure to address the changing environment

Performance Indicators

Metric	Purpose	Suggested approach
Achievement of strategic goals	This is the ultimate validation that ST enabled the organization to reach its strategic outcomes	Directly measure progress toward the strategic objectives that underlie the transformation

Metric	Purpose	Suggested approach
Employee engagement	Ensure that people are embracing the new structure and can work effectively within it	• Gauge employee satisfaction with the new structures • Effectiveness of training programs
Operational performance	Demonstrate tangible business benefits from ST	• Track productivity metrics • Quality indicators • Cost efficiency improvements

Cultural and Behavioral Shifts

Metric	Purpose	Suggested approach
Leadership Effectiveness	Confirm that leaders are operating successfully in the new structure. They are modeling the behaviors required for successful ST	• 360-degree feedback
Collaboration Patterns	Behavioral changes have occurred in how people work together	• Network analysis of reporting lines • Frequency of cross-functional projects • Knowledge sharing behaviors
Change-Readiness	Assess if ST is getting the organization ready for future changes and continuous improvement	• Cultural alignment with new ways of working • Capacity to implement future changes

Key Insights

- **Structural transformation must be strategically driven, not operationally reactive**
  You should be doing this to facilitate the organization's future vision, not patching today's problems. Be clear on the strategic priorities and design a framework to support them.
- **Start with the decision architecture, not organizational charts**
  The biggest changes to structure involve shifting the process for making decisions, who is in charge of what, and how information gets to decision makers. Moving boxes around on an org chart without changing decision rights results in unnecessary costs for the organization (e.g., staff turnover, project disruptions, duplicated/competing efforts), not transformation.

➢ **Get good at building bridges while you're crossing them**
Successful structural transformation improves the existing operations while at the same time preparing for the future. This means coming up with structural solutions that can "walk and chew gum"—maintaining performance while enabling change.

What Not To Do

- ✘ **Treat structural change as a technical exercise rather than a human one**
People's roles, power, and identity will be changed when the structure changes. Engage all of the stakeholders early on to mitigate resistance.
- ✘ **Pursue the perfect structure**
With so much riding on BT, it's easy to see how Leaders get caught up in their quest for the ideal organizational structure. They want to "get it exactly right" before implementing, especially given the disruption involved. This leads to analysis paralysis, delays in changes, and outdated structures, causing employees to lose confidence in leadership's decision-making abilities. One of my mentors told me not to confuse perfection with success. Perfect is the enemy of good—work with iterative changes and continuous improvement.
- ✘ **Fail to define roles, governance and decision rights**
A critical part of structural transformation is to clarify how the new structure is supposed to operate. Specifically:
    - *Who is accountable* for what?
    - *Who has authority* to make which decisions?
    - *How do teams coordinate* across functions, levels, or geographies?

  This omission leads to confusion, inefficiency, power struggles, and ultimately, transformation fatigue.

CHAPTER 6

Cultural Transformation

Figure 6.1 Logo of CT

Complex BTs are vast in scale and scope. They involve simultaneous changes to strategy, business processes, team structures, and digital solutions. They cannot succeed unless the employees understand and agree to the changes.

The culture of the organization determines how its employees perceive and respond to change. Here are a few examples:

1. Cultures that reward innovation tend to embrace change more readily. Risk-averse organizations are resistant to change because they are afraid of failure.
2. Employees who trust their leaders are more likely to support new projects.
3. Agile organizations respond swiftly to change due to a culture of constant adaptation. More structured organizations prefer incremental changes that happen over longer periods of time.

4. Employees that value individualism prioritize change based on personal impact. Employees in a collectivist culture will readily embrace change if there is benefit to the group.

Cultural transformation ensures that change persists beyond surface-level adoption. Training and procedure upgrades can introduce new ways of working, but long-term success necessitates shifting attitudes and behaviors at all levels.

When people feel alienated from the process, they are less likely to accept change. Successful change management promotes engagement tactics that are consistent with cultural values, allowing employees to feel involved and empowered.

Approaching Cultural Transformation

Perform a Culture Gap Analysis

Cultural transformation plays a pivotal role in either accelerating or impeding BT initiatives. It is also the most difficult aspect of BT to undertake. By approaching it systematically, you can navigate this challenging terrain successfully.

- Paint a compelling vision of the kind of culture you want that is aligned with the business strategy and long-term goals of BT. This is the "To Be" culture. State the basic principles that affect decision making and behavior. You also need to tell a clear, memorable narrative to explain what is changing and why. Concrete examples of behavior help turn these ideas into actual strategies, making things clearer and more consistent for employees.
  The "To Be" culture should strike a balance between desire and authenticity. It should support business growth while being true to the organization's history and mission. When done right, this vision becomes both exciting and achievable, motivating teams and making them all the more committed to big changes.
- Next, perform an audit of the current culture. This can be done with surveys, interviews, and focus groups to understand the

organization's main values, beliefs, habits, and unwritten rules. Be alert to subcultures that exist within different departments or regions; this will help to understand the more complex cultural dynamics that you have to address.

- Perform a gap analysis by comparing the results of the culture survey against the traits of the "To Be" culture. Additionally, linking cultural strengths with elements of change guarantees that essential traditions and practices are preserved while supporting change.

Set the Tone at the Top

For cultural transformation to be successful, executives must demonstrate visible, consistent commitment. Executive leadership builds trust and strengthens change by "walking the talk": modeling the behaviors they want to see in others, putting the right resources into the right places, and holding themselves and others accountable for cultural alignment. Talking about cultural goals and progress on a regular basis keeps teams interested and builds trust. When old ways of doing things clash with new principles, leaders have to make tough choices to protect the integrity of the change. If leaders say one thing and do another, their credibility quickly goes down. This shows how important it is for everyone to be fully committed.

Engage the Broader Organization

While Tone at the Top is important for setting the foundation for cultural transformation, long-term success depends on broad-based participation. Identify the cultural change agents at all levels of the organization: the people that are enthusiastic about the changes and have credibility with their peers. Empower them to be cultural ambassadors to help ensure that change is supported by everyone in the organization. Giving employees a say in how the new culture is shaped increases buy-in and ownership. Structured feedback systems help gather important information and concerns. Celebrate early adopters and share success stories to keep the momentum going by showing real progress. By giving teams a place to talk about problems and find solutions together, they can work through obstacles. Cultural transformation becomes truly long-lasting when employees go from being passive recipients to active cocreators.

Align Systems and Structures

To perpetuate the "To Be" culture, stated principles and daily behaviors must align. Checks for cultural fit should be part of the hiring and onboarding processes to make sure everyone is on the same page from the outset. There are a number of tools and techniques to help assess culture and cultural fit: Myers-Briggs Type Indicator (MBTI), DISC (Dominance, Influence, Steadiness, and Compliance) Assessment, Organizational Culture Assessment Instrument (OCAI), and others.

Pay structures should support cultural values, and performance management systems should reward behaviors that are in line with those values. This will make everyone more committed. Career paths should reflect the organization's core values so that people can go up in their careers in a way that supports its mission. The organization should develop a set of Guiding Principles to set the standard for behavior and attitude at work. Lastly, both physical and digital spaces need to make it easier for people to do what they want to do and shape how they interact and get involved.

When cultural messages and organizational incentives are out of synch, people will naturally take actions that lead to tangible results for themselves. Alignment is a key part of long-term change because of this.

Build Change-Readiness

People need to learn new skills and ways of thinking in order to change their culture. Find the capability gaps that stop this from happening. Provide employees with learning experiences that boost their ability to embrace change. Provide safe spaces where people can try out new behaviors to boost their confidence and ability to change. Coaching helps people through change by giving them personalized support.

Make change resilience a core competence so that teams can keep moving forward despite shifting dynamics. Learning shouldn't only happen in formal training. Employees should also have chances to try out new ways of doing things in real-world situations, which will reinforce lasting transformation.

Cultural Transformation Profile: LEGO

LEGO Group is a privately held Danish toy company. Its core product is a line of interlocking building bricks. They also operate LEGOLAND theme parks around the world. In 2017, cultural issues were identified as one contributing factor to a period of stalled growth (Sull and Sull 2025).

Lack of cohesion: A number of different leadership models had evolved over time across the company. Decision making lacked a unified strategic direction. This, in turn, resulted in confusion and inefficiencies, negatively impacting employee engagement.

Top-down leadership: Initiatives were often dictated from the top, rather than developed in collaboration with employees.

In 2018, the "Leadership Playground" framework (LEGO 2021) was created with the objective of fostering a collaborative, innovative and inclusive leadership culture. It was based on three core principles:

Be Brave—Employees are encouraged to challenge the status quo, take ownership of decisions, and stand by their convictions.

Be Curious—Promotes exploration, questioning assumptions, and pushing boundaries to drive innovation.

Be Focused—Helps employees prioritize actions that align with LEGO's mission and long-term goals.

The executive team realized that leadership responsibility needed to be less hierarchical and more distributed to empower their employees at all levels. This framework was intentionally built from the bottom up by LEGO employees.

As a result, LEGO became a more agile company, able to make better decisions. The outcomes they realized are impressive (Sull and Sull 2025).

- LEGO's annual revenue increased by an average of 10 percent over five years, outpacing competitors like Disney, Mattel, and Hasbro, which grew at 3 percent.
- The company maintained industry-leading profitability, demonstrating that its leadership and cultural changes translated into financial success.
- The shift to a more unified leadership model fostered greater collaboration and innovation, helping LEGO stay agile in a competitive market.

Measuring Progress

Set clear targets for both business and cultural results to make sure that changes in behavior are in line with strategic goals. Gather both quantitative and qualitative data for continuing evaluation. Look at new data next to baseline numbers to see clear evidence of change. Connect changes in culture to how they affect operations and finances. This will help everyone involved comprehend how change is benefiting them. Keep people motivated by adapting strategy based on the metrics you're developing.

In the absence of the metrics, it's hard to show the value of cultural transformation. That, in turn, makes it difficult to keep people committed when the inevitable issues arise.

Here is a summary of metrics that can help you assess progress with strategically aligned cultural change.

Employee Engagement

Metric	Purpose	Suggested approach
Employee Engagement	Sets a baseline measure of the employees' commitment to the organization	• Employee engagement surveys • Net Promoter Scores (NPS)
Trust in leadership	Credibility and confidence in the leaders' ability to drive transformation	• Employee engagement surveys
Cultural Alignment	Check if transformation efforts are creating authentic cultural change or superficial adjustments	• Cultural assessment audit

Psychological Safety	Do employees feel secure enough to take risks, speak up and admit mistakes	• Edmondson Psychological Safety Scale

Behavior and Performance

Metric	Purpose	Suggested approach
Collaboration	Determine if silos are breaking down and integration is occurring	• Cross-functional project participation rates • Time to resolve cross-departmental issues • Usage rates of collaboration platforms and tools
Innovation and Risk Taking	Shows if transformation is becoming everyone's concern, not just leadership	• Number of ideas submitted through innovation programs • Percentage of employees participating in improvement initiatives • Rate of experimentation with new approaches or technologies
Accountability	Are employees taking initiative, or waiting for direction	• Goal achievement rates across teams • Quality scores/defect rates • Proactive problem identification

Retention and Attraction

Metric	Purpose	Suggested approach
Turnover Analysis	Provides a broad indicator of employee satisfaction and cultural fit	• Voluntary turnover • Retention of high performers • Exit interview themes • Time-to-fill culture critical roles
Talent Acquisition	Gauge market perception of the organization's culture. Track employee advocacy and confidence in the culture.	• Quality of candidate poll • Cultural fit assessments • Offer acceptance rates • Referral rates from current employees

Communication and Transparency

Metric	Purpose	Suggested approach
Information flow	Identify communication gaps	• Participation in group meetings • Use of internal communication channels • How quickly information cascades through organizational levels

Metric	Purpose	Suggested approach
Feedback	Do communication patterns support desired cultural attributes (e.g., collaboration, trust)	• Frequency of upward feedback to leaders • Quality and frequency of performance conversations • # ideas implemented from employee suggestions

Leadership and Development

Metric	Purpose	Suggested approach
Leadership effectiveness	Are leaders embodying new cultural behaviors	• 360 feedback for managers • Succession planning metrics • Manager retention rates
Learning and growth	Is the organization developing skills needed to sustain cultural transformation over time	• Internal promotion rates • Skills development assessments • Engagement in mentoring programs

Stakeholder Impact

Metric	Purpose	Suggested approach
External reputation	Validates if cultural transformation is enhancing the organization's image and competitive positioning	• Customer satisfaction & loyalty scores • Brand perception • Social media sentiment analysis
Stakeholder relationships	Validates if cultural transformation is positively impacting relationships with stakeholders	• Community engagement levels • Investor confidence • Third-party partner satisfaction ratings

Financial and Operational

Metric	Purpose	Suggested approach
Performance outcomes	Quantify business impact to justify the investment in cultural transformation	• Productivity measures • Cost reduction through cultural initiatives • Revenue from new product and services

Metric	Purpose	Suggested approach
Risk and compliance	Indicates if cultural transformation is strengthening the ethical climate and creating a safe and respectful workplace	• Ethical violation reports • Safety incidents • Audit findings • Insurance claims or litigation related to workplace culture

Key Insights

- **Culture *still* eats strategy for breakfast**
  The original quote attributed to Peter Drucker (Engel 2018) is still relevant. Successful organizations either align their strategies with cultural strengths or invest in cultural transformation as a prerequisite to strategic change. Treating culture as a strategic asset requires as much attention as financial resources or market positioning.
- **"Tone At The Top" is everything**
  Authentic leadership behavior is necessary for cultural change to work. Leaders need to demonstrate the values that they say they want to see in others. When leaders don't act in line with their professed principles, it makes it harder to convince the team to change. Additionally, leaders must be transparent, vulnerable and willing to give up their old ways of leading, if that's what is needed.
- **Cultural transformation is a marathon, not a sprint**
  It takes months, if not years, of dedication to truly change a culture. Deep cultural tendencies are embedded in organizations over decades. Change involves regular reinforcement in hiring, performance measurements, incentive systems, communication, and decision making. Leaders must learn to stay motivated amid plateaus and adapt based on feedback.

What Not To Do

- **Ignore existing cultural strengths**
  Organizations often overlook important cultural elements in their current culture, leading to alienation and resistance. Cultural transformations should preserve elements such as technical expertise, strong customer relationships, and resilience. Successful cultural transformations honor the past, while enabling adaptation for the future.
- **Treat cultural transformation like a PR campaign**
  If cultural change is implemented as a messaging exercise, that will lead to cynicism and skepticism among employees. They need to see real changes to systems, procedures, and leadership behaviors.
- **Avoid addressing structural barriers**
  This is the most common mistake organizations make when pursuing cultural change: they leave organizational structures unchanged. Common issues are performance measurements that go against cultural norms, hierarchies that make it hard to work together, resource allocation systems that don't follow priorities, and promotion criteria that perpetuate behaviors that aren't in line with the "To Be" culture.

CHAPTER 7

Managing BT Risks

Risk management is a best practice in BT that ensures potential threats to success are identified, evaluated, and addressed proactively. BT efforts have some element of uncertainty, which can vary from operational interruption and resistance to change to cost overruns, regulatory noncompliance, and reputational damage. A strong risk management system involves early risk identification and continuous monitoring, allowing organizations to adjust quickly and make informed decisions. This entails mapping strategic, operational, financial, legal, and reputational risks throughout the transformation process and assigning responsibility for mitigating them. Adding risk thinking to BT governance not only protects value, but it also builds confidence among stakeholders, regulators, and executives. Transformation risk becomes a source of strength and an opportunity to outperform the competition.

BT specific risks can be grouped into five categories.

Strategic Misalignment

Organizations often embark on BT initiatives in response to competitive challenges or technology developments without verifying that the effort will satisfy a true business need. BT becomes the "tail that wags the dog." Being out of synch with the business strategy or market realities makes the misalignment more harmful over time when circumstances change, yet BT continues to pursue obsolete goals. As a result, BT initiatives fail to provide real economic value or competitive advantage.

Suggestions for mitigation:

- Conduct stage-gate reviews
  Break the larger BT initiative into manageable phases. After each phase conduct a stage-gate review. These serve as structured

decision points during which you test assumptions, validate that the work still supports the strategic goals, and decide if you need to adjust the scope or BT objectives in response to changes in the business environment or strategy. At each gate, you have the option to continue, stop, or pivot based on current circumstances. Taking this stepwise approach lowers the risk of wasting resources from blindly carrying on despite a change in conditions. It increases governance and accountability and ensures that investments consistently support the changing strategy.

- Define specific, measurable outcomes before starting BT
  These provide clear benchmarks for whether BT is delivering value in accordance with business priorities. When outcomes are tied directly to strategic objectives, it creates an explicit relationship between the team's day-to-day activities and the company's overall direction. Measurable outcomes also serve as an early warning system: If results don't match up with the goals, you can immediately identify misalignment and make modifications before resources are wasted. This clarity not only informs your decision making and resource allocations, but it also strengthens accountability, ensuring that BT remains focused on moving the strategy forward instead of getting sidetracked by irrelevant or low-impact goals.
- Always have an exit strategy
  For large strategic initiatives like BT, having an exit strategy is a critical governance safeguard. If BT no longer aligns with the company's priorities, delivers the intended value, or falls outside the risk appetite, there is a clear, disciplined way to stop or redirect it. An exit strategy demonstrates prudent stewardship of resources and keeps the strategic portfolio focused on what best advances the mission and long-term goals. Exit strategies typically include the following:
  1. Exit Criteria: predefined triggers that let you know when BT should be reconsidered.
  2. Decision Making Authority: Who has the authority to make the stop/pivot decision.

3. Risk and Opportunity Assessment: An evaluation of the risks of continuing versus exiting.
4. Resource Allocation Plan: How you will redirect resources (funding, staff, technology) to other initiatives.
5. Transition and Wind-Down Tasks: Activities to close out contracts and vendor partnerships. You'll also want to preserve intellectual property compiled to date, as well as archive associated data.
6. Communication Strategy: This is a comprehensive plan for what you will tell stakeholders, how you will tell them, and when you will tell them. The key message is to frame the decision as responsible governance.
7. Lessons Learned: Convene the team to capture insights on what worked, what didn't, and how these lessons can be applied to the governance of future initiatives.

People and Change Resistance

The human factor is the most unpredictable and potentially harmful risk in BT. When faced with change, employees may feel anxious about losing their status in the workplace, or their job security. A natural reaction is aggressive or passive resistance that can ruin even well-planned projects. This resistance reveals itself in several ways, such as key employees not being available at important times, teams going back to old methods of doing things even when new mechanisms are in place. The "coconut phone" kicks in (informal networks) to spread negativity that hurts the credibility of leaders. In established businesses, cultural inertia is especially strong because "the way we've always done things" becomes a big part of who employees are and how the organization works.

In addition to resistance, change often reveals skill gaps that weren't obvious when things were running well. People who did well in the past may have trouble grasping the new technologies, techniques, or ways of thinking that are needed to be successful. This has a domino effect on the whole organization, lowering productivity, raising stress levels, and lowering confidence. Leaders often don't realize how much time and money it takes to close these gaps. That leads to unrealistic deadlines and not enough help for staff who must make the change happen.

Suggestions for mitigation:

- Include organizational change management (OCM) from day one
  Ensure that you have lined up visible support from the executive team. In your BT budget, include funding specifically for OCM (I usually allow 15 to 20 percent of the total budget). To make sure that change considerations influence strategic decisions instead of reacting to problems as they arise, do your stakeholder analysis, create comprehensive communication plans, and identify potential points of resistance before major BT decisions are made.
- Involve employees in planning
  Include employees from various levels and departments in planning groups and pilot programs. Being on the front lines, they are in a position to bring up useful insights that senior leaders may miss. Making them a part of the change will give them a sense of ownership.
- Invest in retraining and upskilling programs
  Create learning paths for different jobs and levels of skill that include hands-on training, ongoing coaching, and chances to practice in low-risk settings before full implementation of BT. Make sure that training comes in a variety of forms (e.g., in-person, online, peer mentoring), and that it lasts beyond the initial rollout to support ongoing learning as employees face problems with new systems and processes in the real world.
- Identify and empower change champions throughout the organization
  Select respected, credible employees from various departments and levels to serve as advocates for BT, give peer support, and act as feedback channels between leadership and frontline staff. Give these champions early information, specialized training, dedicated time for change activities, and visible recognition to bolster their role as motivators and influencers with their coworkers.
- Address cultural barriers explicitly through leadership modeling

Leaders must demonstrate the behaviors and mindsets that BT requires. They should use new technology themselves, admit that they too have things to learn, reward the courage to try new ways of doing things, and make sure that sacred cows don't get in the way of transformation goals. This means having candid conversations about aspects of the culture that must change, why they matter, and what will take their place. Successful leaders take a proactive approach to OCM, rather than hope culture will shift organically.

Technology

Technology risks in BT go far beyond just system failures or bugs. When new and old systems don't work well together, it might lead to data discrepancies, workflow bottlenecks, or security holes that weren't planned for. These technical debt problems get worse over time, making maintenance harder and restricting future options. When organizations try to use new technologies, they often find that their current data quality, system architecture, or infrastructure capabilities aren't good enough. This means they must make unplanned investments in repairs that weren't planned for in the first place.

The speed of technology change itself adds to the risk. Solutions that were cutting-edge during planning may not be useful by the time they are implemented. When you rely on a vendor, you are exposed to situations that are not in your control. For example, the vendor buys another company, stops making a product, or changes its support. Another layer of risk to consider is that modern technology ecosystems are so complicated that even minor technical decisions can have big impacts that don't show up until months or years later. This could require costly architecture changes or system overhauls.

Suggestions for mitigation:

- Conduct technical assessments and proof of concepts
  Before you commit to large-scale implementation, run controlled proof-of-concept projects that test the proposed technology against real business scenarios, data volumes and integration

requirements. This will help you validate assumptions and uncover technical limitations early on. Include infrastructure readiness reviews, security audits, and performance tests under conditions that simulate real production environments. This will ensure the solution can handle the complexities of real life.

- Plan for extensive testing phases and rollback procedures
  Set up multilayered testing procedures that include performance testing, user acceptance testing, integration testing, and unit testing. Make sure you have established clear success criteria and enough time is allowed to find and fix problems before production deployment. Create detailed rollback plans that include specific triggers for reverting to previous systems. If major problems arise during implementation, the company can quickly resume operations without data loss or extended down time.
- Ensure robust data backup and security measures
  This may seem obvious, but I can't stress enough the importance of ensuring that your backup approach includes multiple redundant copies of critical data stored in different locations. Regularly test your restoration procedures to verify that backups are functional and complete. Strengthen security protocols to address new vulnerabilities introduced by BT. Among others, this must include updated incident response plans that protect against both external and internal risks during the transition period.
- Choose proven technologies over cutting-edge but unproven solutions
  It's tempting to want to be seen as "leading edge" by embracing emerging technology solutions. But there is a lot to be said about giving more weight to technologies that have a track record, have strong vendor support, and have been used successfully in similar business situations. This approach lowers the chance of encountering undiscovered defects, limited integration options, poor documentation, or vendors who can't provide the support you need when problems appear during critical implementation phases.
- Build in redundancy and fail-safes
  Design system architectures with redundant components so that single points of failure don't bring down critical operations during

or after BT. Create fail-safe mechanisms like automatic fallback, and manual override options that allow human intervention when automated processes run into unexpected situations.

Financial and Resources

Because change initiatives are interconnected, it's hard to predict and control the associated financial risks. When making initial budget projections, people typically use insufficient information and are overly optimistic about how quickly problems will be solved, how many resources will be available, and how well the project will be implemented. As BT progresses, hidden costs emerge: extra license fees, consultation fees for specialized expertise, longer testing periods, or parallel system operations that use more resources than expected. These cost overruns usually happen late in projects when organizations have already put a lot of money into them and face pressure to keep going despite the financial strain.

Risks in resource allocation go beyond the money. They also involve competition for important employees, specialized skills, and the attention of the business. BT projects usually need the most capable employees, which means they get pulled away from their regular duties that support current revenue generation. It's hard to quantify the opportunity cost (which can be large) when the transformation takes longer than expected. Organizations may find themselves unable to adequately support both transformation and regular business operations, forcing trade-offs that could jeopardize either initiative.

Suggestions for mitigation:

- Include contingency buffers in BT budgets
  Use historical data from similar projects, input from professionals that have experienced their own BT journeys, and detailed bottom-up costing to build the base budget. Then add a substantial contingency reserve (I suggest 20 to 30 percent of the base BT budget) to account for the inevitable unknowns and scope adjustments. Establish rules (when and how they can be used) to govern the release of these funds. This ensures that the money will be used for genuine unforeseen issues, and not to make up for poor planning or scope creep.

- Conduct regular financial reviews of BT initiatives
  Set up a process to track actual to planned costs at a granular level. Conduct reviews at least biweekly to identify variances early on, while it is still possible to take meaningful corrective actions. Set up approval thresholds and other mechanisms to ensure that financial decisions receive appropriate oversight and that leaders have visibility into spending trends before small overruns snowball into major problems.
- Monitor ROI metrics continuously and adjust course when needed
  Don't wait until BT is over to evaluate success. Set clear value realization metrics that are linked to business outcomes and monitor these throughout the transformation period. Use these measures to help you decide whether to stop, continue, or adjust. Early course corrections supported by real-time data are far less costly than sticking with methods that aren't delivering expected returns.

Operational Continuity

Business continuity risks during BT are a result of the tension between keeping the current business running while you're making changes that could temporarily break established procedures. Critical business functions must keep running even if systems, procedures, or organizational structures change. This creates coordination challenges especially when changes affect systems that customers use or fundamental business activities that can't be quickly stopped or reversed. During transition periods, when both old and new systems must work simultaneously, the risk is higher since there are more opportunities for things to go wrong.

Because modern businesses are so interconnected, changes in one area can have a ripple effect across the organization. For example, a seemingly minor change to an application could impact reporting, compliance, customer communications, or partner integrations that weren't immediately obvious. Unfortunately, you usually only find out about these dependencies when something goes wrong and an urgent fix situation is created. These situations can divert resources from planned BT initiatives. The problem is made worse by the fact that many businesses don't have complete records of their current operations and how the systems work together. This makes it difficult to predict and prepare for these cascading impacts.

Suggestions for mitigation:

- Maintain parallel systems during critical transition periods
  During the cutover, run both old and new systems simultaneously for an extended period of time. This allows you to verify that the new systems function properly while maintaining the ability to fall back to your proven processes should problems arise. Yes, this is resource intensive, but it's the safety net that will let you keep critical business functions going, while giving the team the time to resolve issues in the new environment before you decommission the old one.
- Ensure key personnel remain available throughout the process
  Secure executive commitment to prevent key staff from being pulled away to other priorities. This commitment should also include:
  - the ability to cross-train backup staff,
  - providing incentives to people whose departure would jeopardize the success of BT, and
  - knowledge transfer and succession planning to ensure that institutional knowledge isn't held by a few people who might leave voluntarily or become unavailable due to illness or other circumstances during the extended period of transformation.
- Plan transformations during lower-activity periods when possible
  Schedule major transformation cutover activities during slower business cycles. This is because fewer transactions and interactions with customers take place during these times, minimizing the impact of potential disruptions. Additionally, these slower business periods usually mean key employees are more available. They can devote their attention to BT activities and rapid problem resolution.
- Create detailed business continuity plans
  We tend to think that business continuity plans (BCPs) are created for the company to be ready to respond to the impact of an external threat, such as a cyberattack, or a natural disaster. BT

can cause business disruptions of similar magnitude. BCPs by their nature identify critical business processes, the maximum acceptable downtime for each function, and outline step-by-step instructions to keep things running. All of the remedies outlined in a BCP (e.g., alternative workflows, manual workarounds, communication protocols) allow you to act expeditiously when a transformation problem occurs without waiting for executive direction or improvising solutions on the spot.

Studies show that over 80 percent of business transformation efforts fail to achieve their objectives (Burke 2024). Poor risk management is a primary contributing factor. Treating risk mitigation as an afterthought or as an unnecessary cost jeopardizes competitive position, employee morale, customer connections, and financial stability. Successful BT incorporates risk assessment and mitigation actions in project governance, allocates adequate resources for contingency planning, and maintains organizational discipline to address emergent risks before they develop into crises. Organizations that recognize risk management as a core competency rather than a compliance exercise are more likely to emerge stronger from transformation initiatives. This is because the ability to anticipate, adapt to, and overcome BT challenges gives them long-term competitive advantage that goes beyond the specific initiative.

CHAPTER 8
Governance

Adjustments to Govern Complex BT

A complex business transformation simultaneously impacts business process, technology, organizational design, and culture. As such, it should be managed as a "Whole System Transformation" (Carter and Sullivan 2012). The approach to governance will need to shift from oversight of a traditional project to a network-based model capable of dealing with complexity and quickly adapting to emerging issues.

These are recommended changes to governance:

Shift from hierarchical to distributed leadership: Traditional top-down governance is inadequate for complex BT because changes occur simultaneously across multiple interrelated components. Instead, assemble a team of empowered change leaders at various system levels who can make decisions and coordinate locally while maintaining strategic alignment.

Use adaptive decision-making structures: Stage-gate processes should be replaced with more flexible governance models that can adapt to new insights and changing conditions. Being more adept means shorter feedback cycles and the ability to pivot initiatives based on what's learned from early interventions.

Have a multistakeholder communications plan: Complex BT requires coordination with multiple stakeholders who themselves hold varying timelines, their own opinions of how success should be measured, and agendas. The new model of governance will facilitate continuous communication among these groups. That will promote a shared vision and encourage collaborative problem-solving.

Take a portfolio view instead of a single project focus: Rather than governing one large initiative, manage a portfolio of interconnected pilots or proof-of-concept tests that can inform and reinforce each other. This requires coordination that strikes a balance between local autonomy with systemwide consistency.

Shift to learning-oriented oversight: Traditional governance is all about making sure that things are done according to predetermined plans. Instead, adopt "learning velocity," i.e., how rapidly insights from interventions can be captured, analyzed, and used to adjust the overall approach.

Longer timeframes and success metrics: Governance structures need to acknowledge that complex BT can run over several years, where benefits may not be immediately quantifiable. This requires patience, adjusting the organization's risk tolerances, and measures that reflect early indicators of systemic change metrics.

Governance Structures

Generally, governance structures will remain the same but just operate with the recommended changes. You will want to make sure that BT governance integrates with existing corporate governance structures. Here are the steps to achieve this.

1. **Map governance interfaces**
   Start by identifying where transformation intersects existing governance domains:
   - **Board Oversight**: Align transformation goals with fiduciary responsibilities and strategic priorities.
   - **Audit & Risk Committees**: Integrate transformation risks into enterprise risk management frameworks.
   - **CSR (Corporate Social Responsibility) and Ethics Committees:** Ensure transformation initiatives reflect stakeholder values and ethical standards. (See Chapter 9 for more on CSR.)
2. **Overlay a governance structure**
   Create a BT governance layer (e.g., a BT Steering Committee) that interfaces with but does not replace existing corporate governance. This BT governance body will address transformation specific decisions, and at the same time ensures alignment with board oversight,

regulatory compliance, and stakeholder responsibility. The BT governance body will be accountable to the board but has been delegated authority to operate with agility.

3. **Define hybrid decision rights**
   Delineate which decisions remain within traditional governance (e.g., legal, compliance, financial reporting) and those that can be handled by the BT governance body (e.g., new operating models, proof-of-concept test cases). This prevents conflicts while ensuring that both systems can function effectively.
4. **Adapt financial and risk management perspectives**
   Traditional risk frameworks may view transformation activities as high risk because they're uncertain and often experimental. Develop separate risk assessment approaches for BT initiatives that account for the greater risk of *not* transforming. This might include portfolio risk management where failures in individual experiments are expected and planned for.
5. **Incorporate BT metrics with existing performance reporting**
   Include indicators that show learning velocity and progress toward the transformation goals. By taking this dual dashboard approach, boards will understand both traditional business performance and transformation progress.
6. **Evolve BT governance**
   Start with BT governance having limited authority. Expand its scope as confidence builds and the existing governance structures adapt. This approach will help to avoid conflict between stability-focused governance and the change-oriented governance that BT requires.

CHAPTER 9

Social Impact of BT

Corporate citizenship is the notion that companies have a responsibility to society. They should support improving the quality of life and standard of living in the communities in which they operate, while still being profitable for their stakeholders.

The expectation that companies must embrace their social responsibility continues to grow. Investors, customers, and employees use their own power to force management to work harder, think more creatively, and act in line with their values or risk negative consequences if they don't share or follow these values.

Every business has basic moral and legal duties. The most successful companies, on the other hand, build a strong foundation of corporate citizenship by balancing the needs of shareholders with those of the community and the environment around them. Research from the Kelly School of Business (Mackin 2020) found that investors place a higher value on firms that are best-in-class in terms of their social responsibility. The brand becomes more attractive to consumers. These companies can better attract high-quality employees. In short, it's not just about doing good—it's about doing well by doing good.

What Is CSR?

CSR is a business strategy that supports a company's goal to be a good corporate citizen, striking that balance between economic performance, ethical behaviors, and social influence.

CSR is often divided into four pillars:

- **Environmental** responsibility entails decreasing pollution, conserving resources, and implementing sustainable practices.
- **Ethical** responsibility means treating employees, customers, and suppliers fairly and transparently.

- **Philanthropic** responsibility is donating to charities, supporting community activities, and encouraging volunteering.
- **Economic** responsibility is making financial decisions that serve both social and environmental objectives.

How does BT Intersect with CSR?

With the right approach, BT can strengthen these pillars, making sure that business growth is beneficial for society. On the other hand, poorly planned or poorly executed BT can have negative consequences.

1. **Environmental Responsibility**
   Environmental sustainability is becoming a more important part of the business process. Transformation initiatives often include switching to greener technologies, lowering carbon footprints, and making supply networks more efficient. For example, organizations who update their logistics or production processes may be able to cut down on waste and emissions by a large amount. DX also helps dematerialization, which means less paper, travel, and energy-intensive work.

   For environmental benefits to occur, design must be intentional. If BT speeds up consumption, encourages planned obsolescence, or ignores the effects of digital waste on the environment, it could do more harm than good. From the start, responsible BT must include environmental sustainability.
2. **Ethical Responsibility**
   Companies must sustain and strengthen ethical norms throughout times of change. Changes in how data is collected, processed, or used (particularly through artificial intelligence [AI] and automation) can put business integrity and consumer trust to the test. To achieve ethical standards, companies must take steps to protect data privacy, fix algorithmic bias, and make governance clear.

   Internally, BT often changes how people operate and how decisions are made. Ethical change means treating employees properly throughout times of change by giving them chances to learn new skills, making sure they understand what's going on, and being there for them when they need it. Ignoring these employer obligations could damage the company's reputation and the confidence of stakeholders.

3. **Philanthropic Responsibility**
Philanthropy is an indicator of a company's commitment to the well-being of the community. When companies use their resources for the public good, BT can amplify those efforts (e.g., using digital platforms to expand outreach to the community, teaching digital skills in schools).

    Some go even further by including a social impact component in their BT goals. For example, make investments to expand their presence in underserved communities, or come up with new ways to make their services accessible for community members. However, short-term financial pressures from BT may lead to a decline in philanthropy. Long-term vision and a real commitment to CSR are demonstrated by continuing to do philanthropic work throughout times of change.

4. **Economic Responsibility**
If a company operates profitably while delivering shareholder value, it is meeting its economic responsibility. BT's goals often focus on improved business efficiency, innovation, and making the company more competitive in the market. Digital platforms, leaner processes, and new revenue streams all support lasting economic growth.

    But BT also needs to consider a holistic view of economic impact. All stakeholders should share the benefits. Putting too much focus on shareholder returns or cost cutting could hurt long-term economic responsibility, especially if it means laying off workers, lowering wages, or taking value out of local communities.

Key Insights

- BT can enhance all four pillars of CSR, but only if it is done with purpose and careful planning. Integrating CSR into the BT strategy ensures that change not only gives your company an edge over its competitors but also strengthens society.

CHAPTER 10

Do You Need a BT Consultant?

The current pace of change means businesses have to deal with complicated problems that need specialized knowledge and new perspectives. While internal teams have valuable institutional knowledge, there are situations where hiring a consultant is not only useful, but necessary for the BT initiative to move forward successfully.

Here are indicators that you need to engage a BT consultant.

Top Five Indicators That You Need a BT Consultant

1. **You're overwhelmed by the speed of technological change**
   The speed of technological innovation is unparalleled. Technologies such as cloud computing, artificial intelligence, machine learning, quantum computing, and IoT are disrupting industries. It's becoming harder for companies to stay current. For many companies, this flood of ideas causes paralysis because leaders know they must change but can't decide which technologies they should invest in, much less what those investments look like.

   A consultant with expertise in digital transformation contributes knowledge from many different industries and use cases. They can rapidly assess the digital maturity of your company, identify key areas for improvement, and suggest transformation approaches that are in line with the company's goals. More crucially, they can convert difficult technical ideas into business value propositions that executives can understand.

   Consultants also have relationships with technology vendors and implementation experts, which gives them quick access to resources that would take the company years to build in-house. Their experience helps businesses avoid common pitfalls and speeds up the adoption rates of change.

2. **You need an impartial, unbiased opinion**
   Within organizations, internal politics, personal agendas, and historical precedents often become roadblocks for decision making. When BT requires challenging choices about strategic pivots, departmental restructuring, or resource allocation, these biases can derail even the most brilliant projects.

   External consultants provide objectivity that internal stakeholders just cannot match. They provide honest judgments based on facts and business results, without worrying about the office politics or their own careers.

   This neutrality is especially useful for assessing departments that are underperforming, seeing how well leaders are performing, and evaluating whether old processes and systems should be removed. Because the consultant is a neutral third party, they can help people have difficult conversations that they would otherwise avoid. They can create safe spaces for productive conflict, ensuring that everyone's opinions are heard and that discussions stay focused on the organization's goals and not on personal issues.

3. **You're stalled on how to achieve effective change**
   Many BT projects begin with high energy but rapidly lose steam when teams begin to resist the changes, or when there are problems with implementation. When progress stalls, there is often a never-ending cycle of meetings and debates to "get back on track" without anything being accomplished.

   Breaking through these barriers is what BT consultants do best. They have tried-and-true methods for managing change in organizations. Their toolkit includes techniques for effectively involving stakeholders, communication frameworks, risk mitigation approaches, and implementation roadmaps that can be tailored to your particular situation.

   Consultants also provide systems of accountability to keep transformation initiatives under control. Frequent evaluations, performance reviews, and reaching milestones keep the transformation momentum going, and show value throughout the transformation process. Because of their experience, consultants identify problems before they materialize, which lets them apply proactive actions.

4. **You recognize that you lack in-house expertise**
When a company undertakes complex business transformation, it typically needs expertise that doesn't already exist internally. Whether you're building new business models, restructuring supply chains, or using advanced analytics, you could need skills that your current staff lacks.

   BT consultants give you immediate access to specialized knowledge, so you can avoid making investments in hiring and recruiting people for demands that are only temporary. These professionals bring frameworks and methods that have been refined by working with many clients. Your organization benefits from these best practices without the learning curve.

   BT consultants also collaborate with your team to transfer knowledge throughout the engagement. This approach builds internal skills while also accomplishing the transformation goals. The right consultant helps your team get better at sustaining the change, and ensures they can continue to build on the transformation results long after they depart.

5. **Your stakeholders don't trust you**
As we've seen, a wide range of people, including board members, employees, customers, and investors, need to support your BT efforts. It's critical to build and keep their trust so that you can get the resources to keep things progressing when the inevitable challenges arise.

   Engaging reputable BT consultants shows that the company is serious about making real changes. Their experience and professional reputation provide them with credibility that helps allay investor fears regarding risk and ROI. When change calls for a large financial investment, or deviates from traditional business practices, validation from acknowledged experts can be especially powerful.

   Consultants' experience in stakeholder management lets them customize communications for different audiences, ensuring that everyone from frontline staff to board members knows how transformation projects align with their interests and the organization's strategic goals.

What to Look for in a BT Consultant

The ideal BT consultant combines functional expertise with interpersonal skills that mesh with your organization's unique needs. Here are suggestions for your evaluation checklist.

Expertise and Experience

Industry Knowledge	• Demonstrates understanding of your industry's specific challenges • Has worked with organizations similar in size and complexity • Is current with relevant industry trends and regulations *Note: Strongly aligned experience and expertise in an industry is a good thing. But sometimes outside thinking can help you break through innovation log jams, especially where industries tend to be somewhat insular and get ingrained in how they do things. For example, my experience in online financial services helped a legacy media company develop a multichannel strategy for their products, thus preventing further erosion of their business.*
Transformation Experience	• Has led similar transformation initiatives successfully • Provides relevant case studies with measurable outcomes • Demonstrates experience with your specific transformation needs
Technical Expertise	• Shows proficiency in technologies relevant to your transformation • Balances technical knowledge with business acumen • Demonstrates understanding of integration challenges
Methodology Approach	• Presents clear, structured methodology for transformation • Adapts approach based on organizational needs rather than using rigid frameworks • Shows evidence of continuous improvement in their methods

Strategic Capabilities

Problem Analysis	• Asks insightful questions about your business challenges • Quickly identifies core issues versus symptoms • Demonstrates analytical rigor in approach to problems
Solution Development	• Proposes innovative yet practical solutions • Considers multiple alternatives before recommending approach • Tailors recommendations to your specific context
Systems Thinking	• Considers interconnections between different business areas • Anticipates potential ripple effects of proposed changes • Addresses root causes rather than superficial issues
Risk Management	• Proactively identifies potential risks in transformation • Presents mitigation strategies for identified risks • Has contingency planning built into approach

Implementation Capabilities

Project Management	• Demonstrates strong track record of on-time, on-budget delivery • Presents clear project governance structure • Shows effective resource allocation in previous projects
Change Management	• Presents comprehensive approach to managing resistance • Has strategies for stakeholder engagement at all levels • Demonstrates experience with culture change initiatives
Results Measurement	• Proposes clear KPIs and success metrics • Has systems for tracking progress and outcomes • Shows evidence of delivering measurable results in past projects
Knowledge Transfer	• Has specific plans for building internal capabilities • Creates comprehensive documentation and training materials • Focuses on sustainable results after engagement ends

Communication and Collaboration

Communication Skills	• Articulates complex concepts clearly and concisely • Tailors communication style to different audiences • Produces high-quality written materials and presentations
Stakeholder Management	• Has strategies for engaging executive leadership • Shows ability to connect with frontline employees • Demonstrates political savvy in navigating organizations
Team Integration	• Works effectively with internal teams • Balances leading and supporting roles appropriately • Demonstrates cultural sensitivity and adaptability
Listening Skills	• Actively listens and incorporates feedback • Asks clarifying questions before offering solutions • Shows genuine interest in understanding your perspective

Professional Attributes

Integrity and Ethics	• Transparent about capabilities and limitations • Discloses potential conflicts of interest • References confirm trustworthiness and integrity
Adaptability	• Shows flexibility when circumstances change • Can pivot strategy based on emerging information • Demonstrates creative problem-solving when faced with obstacles
Independence	• Willing to challenge assumptions and present alternative views • Not influenced by vendor relationships or other external factors • Maintains objectivity in recommendations

Cultural Fit	• Aligns with your organizational values and culture • Working style complements your internal team dynamics • Demonstrates genuine interest in your organization's success

Commercial Terms

Value for Investment	• Fees are appropriate for expertise and scope • Clear correlation between costs and deliverables • Demonstrates ROI potential that justifies investment
Contract Structure	• Offers flexible engagement models • Has clear performance guarantees or shared risk components • Transparent about all costs and potential additional fees
Resource Allocation	• Assigns appropriate level of resources to our project • Balances senior oversight with efficient staffing model • Transparent about which team members will be involved
Availability and Timeline	• Can meet our required timeline and milestones • Has necessary availability for our project demands • Realistic about timeline expectations`

Note: Your checklist is intended to be used as part of a comprehensive selection process that includes reference checks, proposal reviews, and in-person interviews with the BT consultant and their team members.

CHAPTER 11

Where Do You Go from Here?

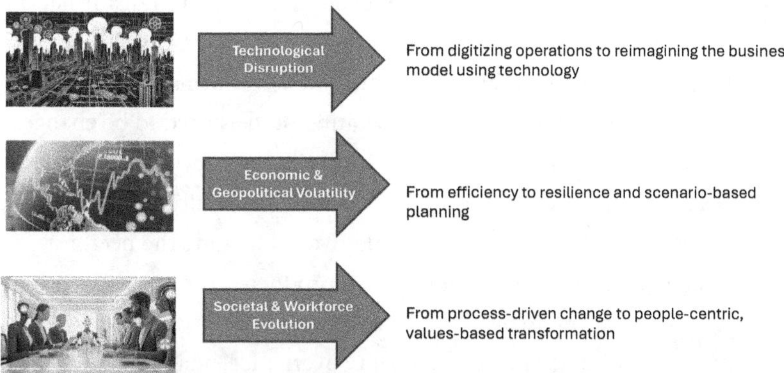

Figure 11.1 Environmental forces impacting BT

Pace of Change and Implications to Organizations

Embrace Change or Risk Extinction

The business world is changing at an exponential pace, driven by emerging technologies, shifting customer needs, new competitors, and more. Organizations that are flexible and open to change will thrive. Those that can't, or won't adjust, risk becoming obsolete. Organizations that proactively plan for the future instead of just reacting to change will have a long-term competitive edge. It's important to be open to changing business models, applying new technologies, and experimenting with new ideas. Organizations can make real progress, have an impact, and flourish by seeing change as an opportunity instead of a threat.

Real-World Challenges

There are three significant forces impacting the current business environment, which, in turn, influence how organizations approach BT.

Here is an expanded explanation of the specific impact each environmental force has on BT.

1. **Technological Disruption**
   - New technologies like AI, quantum computing, and edge computing require businesses to execute faster digital transformation to stay competitive and relevant (Manyika and Chui 2013).
   - Legacy systems can't easily adapt to new platforms or data needs; hence, IT architectures and operating models need to be changed.
   - Technology disruption makes it possible for new models to emerge that need adjustments to structures, cultures, and processes (Accelare 2023). Examples would include the need for new platforms, or moving from a product-centric to a service-centric focus.
   - Companies need to embed data governance, analytics, and AI governance into their daily operations.

     BT Implication: Leaders need to make technology more than a business enabler; they need to make it a strategic driver. The transformation strategy needs to be flexible to take advantage of emerging innovations.
2. **Economic and Geopolitical Volatility**
   - Supply chain shocks, inflation, and trade restrictions change the focus from lean efficiency to adaptability and redundancy.
   - Rising interest rates, unstable markets, and geopolitical risks (e.g., tensions between China and the United States, regional wars) can delay BT projects, or lead to reallocation of BT budgets for other purposes.
   - Trade barriers and regulatory nationalism mean that operations, sourcing, and compliance models need to change.
   - Boards are demanding better risk management for BT. This would include scenario planning and dynamic governance (Murray and Reul 2022).

BT Implication: Resilience and geopolitical adaptation must now be built into the core design of BT, not as an afterthought.

3. **Societal Change and Workforce Evolution**
   - Employees want flexibility, purpose, and fairness. This changes the way organizations are set up, how they work, and how they lead.
   - Gaps in skills in emerging technology slows down transformation. New ways for employees to learn and grow must be designed.
   - Corporate social responsibility (CSR) and sustainability are now key drivers of BT that affect strategy and relationships with stakeholders.
   - Millennials and Gen Z put a lot of value on digital fluency, diversity, and ethical governance. This puts pressure on businesses to accelerate modernization.
   - The rise of AI and humanoid systems in the workplace will require leaders to think about not only how we work but what work means, and the human impact.

   BT Implication: BT must take a "people first" approach. Be mindful of the change fatigue impacting employees. Workforce planning must be a part of BT initiatives from the start.

What BT Will Look Like in the Future

As the pace of change continues to accelerate, businesses will modify their approach to BT. They will move away from traditional, multiyear linear change toward more flexible, iterative, and resilient transformation models.

Strategic planning cycles are getting shorter: two to three years compared to five to ten years. This allows for more frequent assessments of emerging trends, disruptions and opportunities, that lead to faster adaptation.

As strategy cycles get shorter, BT will change from a large one-time event to a core capability. Structures, processes, and technologies will be constantly adjusted to stay ahead of fast-changing conditions.

CURRENT BT	ADAPTABLE BT
▪ Longer strategy horizon	❖ 2–3 year strategy cycles
▪ Linear, sequential planning	❖ Continuous reassessment
▪ One-time, large-scale initiatives	❖ Iterative planning and execution
▪ Centralized control & governance	❖ Ongoing, modular transformation waves
▪ Slow adaption to change	❖ Empowered teams and decentralized decision making
	❖ Parallel, dynamic planning
	❖ Fast feedback loops
	❖ Data-driven pilots

Figure 11.2 BT model shift

To succeed with this new adaptable BT model, organizations must "get comfortable with being uncomfortable." Leaders will need to create a culture of adaptability. What does that look like? A safe and supportive environment is provided to help employees feel comfortable with change. Cross-departmental cooperation is the norm following agile principles of quickly iterating, and getting feedback.

Governance systems need to be more flexible so that decisions can be reached and changes can be made more quickly. Organizations also need to use real-time data and feedback to steer their BT initiatives in a way that keeps them in line with their strategic goals.

A caveat regarding the accelerated pace of change. Leaders must be aware of the danger of "change whiplash" impacting employees. For the most part, people will cope if they can see a path of continuous improvement. They will feel like things are moving forward. If they perceive that they're moving backward and forward, it will be demoralizing.

Summary: Top 10 Causes of BT Failures

The reality is that 88 percent of business transformation efforts fail (Burke 2024). The top 10 reasons for failure are the following:

1. **The "Why" isn't clear**
   When employees do not understand the "why" behind the changes they are being asked to make, anxiety, cynicism, and resistance set

in. All transformations require support from the people involved. It is imperative that a clear and compelling case for change is made. The message cannot be based solely on the financial benefits to the organization, but focusing on why change is necessary, how it will affect them, and how they will "win."

2. **There is no cohesive strategy**
   Business transformation must be established within the context of a clearly defined organizational strategy. However, many organizations struggle to define the role of transformation in driving that strategy.
3. **The executive team are misaligned**
   When the executive team is not aligned on the goals and approach to transformation, it creates confusion throughout the organization. Mixed messages promulgated by different executives undermine credibility and create competing priorities. The leadership teams below the executive level are subject to conflicting directives, leading to paralysis, frustration, and inconsistent execution. Communication is vital!
4. **Core business issues aren't being addressed**
   A core business issue is a problem with a key part of the business. Some organizations mistakenly use transformation as a way to avoid dealing with basic business problems. It's akin to remodeling a house without addressing the cracked foundation. An example of a core business issue is market misalignment, where strategies, capabilities, resources, and management structures are not aligned. Without confronting those underlying issues, any benefit from the BT is short-lived.
5. **There is no change management plan**
   Throughout this book we refer to change management, the pace of change, change fatigue—for good reason. There is a tendency to focus on the structural and process changes for BT, while neglecting the people and cultural implications. You must be intentional in engaging all stakeholders to evolve culture, values, and mindsets to avoid undermining transformation efforts. Failing to effectively manage change will kill your BT initiative.
6. **Performance metrics are not clear**
   Without clear measurable objectives that are linked to business outcomes, teams will have difficulty prioritizing their work and

maintaining momentum. Without specific metrics to track the progress of transformation, it will be difficult to demonstrate value and justify the continued investment.

7. **Insufficient resources and capabilities**
   Workforce planning is often marginalized in BT. It is a very common situation for teams to be expected to drive transformation while maintaining "business as usual." Without additional support and resources, both suffer. In the case of DX (digital transformation), workforce planning takes on more importance for the highly in-demand skills involved. Another vital leadership requirement is the ability to prioritize effectively and avoid burning out team members.
8. **Insufficient investment in developing people for success**
   Business transformations always alter the nature of "the work." A primary cause of people resisting change is the fear that they will not be able to be successful in the new organization. Executives must make an upfront commitment to providing professional development to people to be successful in the posttransformation world. Development activities must be built into staff capacity models to ensure that it isn't something that people are required to do on their own time.
9. **Focus is short term**
   It is an intractable problem facing all organizations in the current business environment: the pressure to deliver short-term results, often coming from boards and investors. This leads to prioritizing short-term results over sustainable change. Transformations require sustained commitment to achieve lasting impact.
10. **Weak program management**
    Transformations consist of many moving parts. Multiple workstreams must be coordinated, multidisciplinary teams must be organized, and task interdependencies must be identified and tracked. In the absence of strong program governance, the work becomes fragmented, schedules slip, and cost overruns occur. Issues won't be caught until they become crises.

Summary: Best Practices to Achieve BT

Your ability to provide clear responses to three basic questions will determine your chances of achieving success in BT (or any major change program):

1. Where are we going?
2. How are we going to work together?
3. What needs to be done?

Confirm that BT Links to the Organization's Strategy and Has a Strong Business Case

When the BT initiative clearly supports the organization's overall strategy, and is in line with its mission and vision, it is strategically aligned. A compelling business case should demonstrate how the transformation would bring about both quantitative and qualitative advantages, while maintaining an acceptable risk profile. The supporting assumptions for the business case must be reasonable and based on trustworthy data sources.

Line Up the Senior Leadership Team

Leading BT requires very different skills than leading a business or unit in steady-state or even a smaller, more focused change effort. Transformations are, by definition, comprehensive makeovers of how work is done. Leading these kinds of activities means making progress on a number of projects or workstreams that not only need to be managed in a traditional sense but also need to be brought together in ways that demand a lot of collaboration and difficult choices. Only the senior leadership team can do this work.

Initiate the OCM Program

OCM is a structured approach to bridge the functional and technical aspects of change with the human element of change. Stakeholder engagement, levels of resistance, cultural gaps, and professional development needs are some of the things to address in an OCM program (cf. Overview, note about OCM). The success of OCM relies on the executives providing visible and vocal support for BT.

Engage All Stakeholders Early and Often

In line with OCM, promote open dialogue and build trust through transparent communication. Information from the OCM analysis is critical input for the BT communications plan that outlines who must be addressed, what messages are important, and how the messages are best delivered.

Be Intentional About Technology and Data

Together, technology and data are key to making BT successful and ensure that the effects of transformation last. Choose fit-for-purpose technology solutions because they support specific BT objectives, rather than adopting tools because they are new or popular. A robust data strategy and supporting data governance processes provide executives with the tools to keep track of progress, spot risks, and adapt in real time. Equally important is to embed cybersecurity and digital trust in the BT solutions architecture from the start.

Plan for Sustainability

To achieve sustainable growth during BT, you need to develop a strategy that goes beyond the initial wave of innovation and change. Successful organizations don't look at BT as a one-time event. Instead, they integrate it into their operations, by changing behaviors, systems, and mindsets across every level. Leaders put long-term value ahead of short-term wins by focusing on their social obligations to their stakeholders. The end result is they are not only resilient but will remain relevant through times of uncertainty and disruption.

References

Accelare. 2023. "How Digital Disruption Impacts Businesses: Ways & Examples." November 30. https://www.accelare.com/blog/how-digital-disruption-impacts-businesses-ways-examples/.

Anthony, Scott D., Alasdair Trotter, and Evan Schwarz. 2019. "The Top 20 Business Transformations of the Last Decade." *Harvard Business Review*, September 24. https://hbr.org/2019/09/the-top-20-business-transformations-of-the-last-decade.

Blanding, Michael. 2018. "Amazon vs Whole Foods: When Cultures Collide." *Harvard Business School*, May 14.https://www.library.hbs.edu/working-knowledge/amazon-vs-whole-foods-when-cultures-collide.

Blumberg, Sven, Rahul Das, Jens Lansing, Nils Motsch, Bjorn Munstermann, and Rob Patenge. 2022. "Demystifying Digital Dark Matter: A New Standard to Tame Technical Debt." *McKinsey*, June 23. https://www.mckinsey.com/capabilities/mckinsey-digital/our-insights/demystifying-digital-dark-matter-a-new-standard-to-tame-technical-debt/.

Burke, Melissa. 2024. "88% of Business Transformations Fail to Achieve their Original Ambitions; Those that Succeed Avoid Overloading Top Talent." *Bain & Company*, April 15. https://www.bain.com/about/media-center/press-releases/2024/88-of-business-transformations-fail-to-achieve-their-original-ambitions-those-that-succeed-avoid-overloading-top-talent/.

Businesswire. 2020. "Ecolab's 2030 Impact Goals Advance Sustainable and Productive Operations to Help Industry Achieve Greater Purpose." July 15. https://www.businesswire.com/news/home/20200715005428/en/Ecolabs-2030-Impact-Goals-Advance-Sustainable-and-Productive-Operations-to-Help-Industry-Achieve-Greater-Purpose/.

Carter, Louis, and Roland Sullivan. 2012. "Whole Systems Transformation: The New Paradigm in Strategic Change for the 21st Century." *Best Practices Institute*, January 1.https://www.bestpracticeinstitute.org/images/ls_references/ls_780/WST_FINAL_LRC_FINAL.pdf.

Colvin, Geoff. 2022. "How Amazon Grew an Awkward Side Project into AWS, a Behemoth That's Now 4 Times Bigger Than Its Original Shopping Business." *Fortune*, November 30. https://fortune.com/longform/amazon-web-services-ceo-adam-selipsky-cloud-computing/.

De Leon, Riley. 2022. "Airbnb Survived Covid, But the Crisis Mode in 'Sharing' Economy Stays." *CNBC*, February 3. https://www.cnbc.com/2022/02/03/airbnb-survived-covid-but-the-crisis-mode-in-sharing-economy-stays.html/.

Engel, Jacob M. 2018. "Why Does Culture 'Eat Strategy for Breakfast'?" *Forbes*, November 20. https://www.forbes.com/councils/forbescoachescouncil/2018/11/20/why-does-culture-eat-strategy-for-breakfast/.

Hensel, Anna. 2020. "Inside Ikea's E-Commerce Strategy." *Modern Retail*, March 12. https://www.modernretail.co/retailers/ikea-is-launching-an-e-commerce-app/

LEGO. 2021. "How Does the Leadership Playground Make Our People Feel?" May 19. https://www.lego.com/en-at/careers/stories/leadership-playground?locale=en-at/.

Mackin, Teresa. 2020. "Does Corporate Social Responsibility Pay Off?" *Kelley School of Business Indianapolis*, March 2. https://blog.kelley.indianapolis.iu.edu/2020/03/02/does-corporate-social-responsibility-pay-off/.

Manyika, James, and Michael Chui. 2013. "Disruptive Technologies: Advances That Will Transform Life, Business, and the Global Economy." *McKinsey Global Institute*, May 1. https://www.mckinsey.com/capabilities/mckinsey-digital/our-insights/disruptive-technologies/.

Matuntuta, Simamkele. 2025. "What Is Cognitive Load Theory? Benefits & Applications." *Cloud Assess*, October 3. https://cloudassess.com/blog/what-is-cognitive-load-theory/.

Murray, Malcolm, and Laura Reul. 2022. "Why Dynamic Risk Governance Starts with Shared Data." *Gartner*, May 6. https://www.gartner.com/en/articles/why-dynamic-risk-governance-starts-with-shared-data/.

Oxford Executive Institute. 2024. "Case Study: Netflix's Transition from DVD Rental to Streaming." November 24. https://oxfordexecutive.co.uk/case-study-netflixs-transition-from-dvd-rental-to-streaming/.

Richter, Felix. 2025. "AWS Stays Ahead as Cloud Market Accelerates." *Statista*, November 4. https://www.statista.com/chart/18819/worldwide-market-share-of-leading-cloud-infrastructure-service-providers/.

Stackpole, Thomas. 2021. "Inside Ikea's Digital Transformation." *Harvard Business Review*, June 4. https://hbr.org/2021/06/inside-ikeas-digital-transformation?autocomplete=true.

Sull, Donald, and Charles Sull. 2025. "How the Lego Group Built Culture Change: From the Ground Up." *MIT Sloan Management Review*, January 10. https://sloanreview.mit.edu/article/how-the-lego-group-built-culture-change-from-the-ground-up/.

The Strategy Institute. 2024. "Starbucks International Strategy—A Case Study for Global Success." September 20. https://www.thestrategyinstitute.org/insights/starbucks-international-strategy-a-case-study-for-global-success/.

Westerman, George, D. Bonnet, and A. McAfee. 2014. "The Nine Elements of Digital Transformation." *MIT Sloan Management Review*, January 7. https://sloanreview.mit.edu/article/the-nine-elements-of-digital-transformation/.

Yohn, Denise Lee. 2020. "How Airbnb Survived the Pandemic—And How You Can Too." *Forbes*, November 10. https://www.forbes.com/sites/deniselyohn/2020/11/10/how-airbnb-survived-the-pandemic--and-how-you-can-too/.

About the Author

Caren Shiozaki is a partner with Fortium Partners, the leading provider of interim and fractional technology C-suite leadership. She brings over 20 years of executive experience at Fortune 1000 corporations to Fortium's clients. In addition to serving in various interim C-Suite roles, she also provides board and C-suite advisory services in governance, risk, and compliance. Caren has served as an advisor to venture capital groups and served on the board of a start-up technology company.

A Certified e-Discovery Professional, she also holds professional certifications in corporate governance, data privacy, and business ethics and compliance. Caren is an active philanthropist supporting nonprofit organizations focusing on girls' and women's issues, childhood education, and animal welfare.

Index

www.ingramcontent.com/pod-product-compliance
Lightning Source LLC
LaVergne TN
LVHW020648100826
845148LV00012B/2376

* 9 7 8 1 6 0 6 4 9 1 8 4 3 *